Indochina Monographs

Leadership

by

General Cao Van Vien

U.S. ARMY CENTER OF MILITARY HISTORY

WASHINGTON, D.C.

Library of Congress Cataloging in Publication Data

Vien, Cao Van.
　　Leadership.

　　(Indochina monographs)
　　Supt. of Docs. no.: D 114.18:L46
　　1. Vietnam. Quan lục--Officers--History.
2. Command of troops. I. Title. II. Series.
UB415.V53V53　　　355.3'304'09597　　80-607941

Reprinted 1984

CMH PUB 92-12

This book is not copyrighted and may be reproduced in
whole or in part without consulting the publisher

Indochina Monographs

This is one of a series published by the U.S. Army Center of Military History. They were written by officers who held responsible positions in the Cambodian, Laotian, and South Vietnamese armed forces during the war in Indochina. The General Research Corporation provided writing facilities and other necessary support under an Army contract with the Center of Military History. The monographs were not edited or altered and reflect the views of their authors--not necessarily those of the U.S. Army or the Department of Defense. The authors were not attempting to write definitive accounts but to set down how they saw the war in Southeast Asia.

Colonel William E. Le Gro, U.S. Army, retired, has written a forthcoming work allied with this series, Vietnam: From Cease-Fire to Capitulation. Another book, The Final Collapse by General Cao Van Vien, the last chairman of the South Vietnamese Joint General Staff, will be formally published and sold by the Superintendent of Documents.

Taken together these works should provide useful source materials for serious historians pending publication of the more definitive series, the U.S. Army in Vietnam.

JAMES L. COLLINS, JR.
Brigadier General, USA
Chief of Military History

INDOCHINA MONOGRAPHS

TITLES IN THE SERIES
(title--author/s--LC Catalog Card)

The Cambodian Incursion--Brig. Gen. Tran Dinh Tho--79-21722 — CMH PUB 92-4

The Easter Offensive of 1972--Lt. Gen. Ngo Quang Truong--79-20551 — CMH PUB 92-13

The General Offensives of 1968-69--Col. Hoang Ngoc Lung--80-607931 — CMH PUB 92-6

Intelligence--Col. Hoang Ngoc Lung--81-10844/AACR2 — CMH PUB 92-14

The Khmer Republic at War and the Final Collapse--Lt. Gen. Sak Sutsakhan--79-607776 — CMH PUB 92-5

Lam Son 719--Maj. Gen. Nguyen Duy Hinh--79-607101 — CMH PUB 92-2

Leadership--General Cao Van Vien--80-607941 — CMH PUB 92-12

Pacification--Brig. Gen. Tran Dinh Tho--79-607913 — CMH PUB 92-11

RLG Military Operations and Activities in the Laotian Panhandle--Brig. Gen. Soutchay Vongsavanh--81-10934/AACR2 — CMH PUB 92-19

The RVNAF--Lt. Gen. Dong Van Khuyen--79-607963 — CMH PUB 92-7

RVNAF and U.S. Operational Cooperation and Coordination--Lt. Gen. Ngo Quang Truong--79-607170 — CMH PUB 92-16

RVNAF Logistics--Lt. Gen. Dong Van Khuyen--80-607117 — CMH PUB 92-17

Reflections on the Vietnam War--General Cao Van Vien and Lt. Gen. Dong Van Khuyen--79-607979 — CMH PUB 92-8

The Royal Lao Army and U.S. Army Advice and Support--Maj. Gen. Oudone Sananikone--79-607054 — CMH PUB 92-10

The South Vietnamese Society--Maj. Gen. Nguyen Duy Hinh and Brig. Gen. Tran Dinh Tho--79-17694 — CMH PUB 92-18

Strategy and Tactics--Col. Hoang Ngoc Lung--79-607102 — CMH PUB 92-15

Territorial Forces--Lt. Gen. Ngo Quang Truong--80-15131 — CMH PUB 92-9

The U.S. Adviser--General Cao Van Vien, Lt. Gen. Ngo Quang Truong, Lt. Gen. Dong Van Khuyen, Maj. Gen. Nguyen Duy Hinh, Brig. Gen. Tran Dinh Tho, Col. Hoang Ngoc Lung, and Lt. Col. Chu Xuan Vien--80-607108 — CMH PUB 92-1

Vietnamization and the Cease-Fire--Maj. Gen. Nguyen Duy Hinh--79-607982 — CMH PUB 92-3

The Final Collapse--General Cao Van Vien--81-607989 — CMH PUB 90-26

Preface

War and politics posed many challenges to South Vietnam's military leadership. Unlike his counterpart in some countries, the Vietnamese military commander was not simply a leader of men in combat. Depending on the level of command, he had to play his part in national politics, be himself a grass roots politician, or engage in political warfare. To achieve success, he was often expected to possess several qualities not always required of a professional military leader. The requirements of leadership, therefore, sometimes transcended the conventional framework of accepted rules and principles.

Given these requirements and the fallability of human nature, it had not always been easy to evaluate the total performance of our leadership. The dilemma we faced was that while professional competence during actual combat was a critical criteria, we could not tolerate deliberate aberations in moral and social codes.

In my analysis of the successes and failures of our leadership, I have endeavored to be fair and objective. If I seem to be laudatory of some officers while critical of others, it is not my intention to embarrass any individual. Performance has been the sole basis for all of my evaluations.

This monograph would have been incomplete without the valuable contributions of my colleagues. I am particularly indebted to Lieutenant General Ngo Quang Truong, former I Corps commander, for his assistance concerning ARVN performance during the 1972 Easter Offensive, and to Brigadier General Tran Dinh Tho for a similar report on the Cambodian Incursion, on whose basis I have built several illustrative cases of leadership. To Lieutenant General Dong Van Khuyen, former Chief of Staff of the JGS and Commander, Central Logistics Command, Major General Nguyen Duy Hinh, former Commander, 3d ARVN Infantry Division and Colonel Hoang Ngoc Lung, former Assistant Chief of Staff for Intelligence, JGS, I am grateful for their critical comments and constructive suggestions.

I am also personally indebted to Lieutenant Colonel Chu Xuan Vien and Ms. Pham Thi Bong. Lt. Colonel Vien, the last Army Attache serving at the Vietnamese Embassy in Washington, D.C., has done a highly professional job of translating and editing that helps impart unity of style and organization to the manuscript. Ms. Bong, a former Captain in the Republic of Vietnam Armed Forces and also a former member of the Vietnamese Embassy staff, spent long and arduous hours typing, editing, and in the administrative preparation of my manuscript in final form.

McLean, Virginia
7 July 1978

Cao Van Vien
General, ARVN

Contents

Chapter	Page
I. INTRODUCTION	1
A Millenary Tradition of Military Leadership	1
Birth of the Vietnamese National Army	7
A French Legacy	12
II. LEADERSHIP UNDER PRESIDENT DIEM'S REGIME	20
Background	20
Training and Leadership Development in the RVNAF	33
Operations Against the Binh Xuyen and Rebellious Religious Sects	41
Performance of the 7th Division in the Battle of Ap Bac	52
Military Province Chiefs	55
Small-Unit Leadership	56
Observations	57
III. LEADERSHIP DURING THE PERIOD OF THE DIRECTORATE	62
Background	62
Manpower and Training	67
I Corps and the 1st Infantry Division During the 1966 Buddhist Crisis	74
Military Province Chiefs	82
Airborne Night Raid Against a Communist Base	83
Observations	88
IV. LEADERSHIP DURING PRESIDENT THIEU'S ERA	95
Background	95
The Challenge of Vietnamization	101
The Challenge of Peace	111
The Challenge of Corruption	117
Leadership at the Corps Level: III and IV Corps During the Cambodian Incursion	123
Leadership at the Corps Level: I Corps During the 1972 Easter Offensive	129
Leadership at the Corps Level: II Corps During the Redeployment from Kontum-Pleiku	140

Chapter	Page

    Leadership at the Division Level: The 23d Division's Defense of Kontum 148
    The Leadership of the Province Chiefs of Binh Dinh, Thua Thien and Khanh Hoa 156
    A Battalion Commander: Tong Le Chan 159

V. SUMMARY AND CONCLUSIONS 162

Appendix
    A. Sources of Vietnam's Nationalist Tradition 172
    B. Small Unit Commander's Handbook, 1966 177

GLOSSARY 200

Charts

No.
1. Organization—Vietnamese Armed Forces, 1955 40

Maps

1. Operation in Rung Sat 46
2. Battle of Thuong Phuoc 85
3. The Relief of Kompong Cham (TOAN THANG 42, Phase V) . . . 124
4. Operation CUU LONG 1, 2, 3, IV Corps 128
5. The Defense of Quang Tri, 2 April 1972 131
6. I Corps Counteroffensive 136
7. The II Corps Withdrawal from Pleiku-Kontum, March 1975 . . 142
8. The Defense of Kontum 150

CHAPTER I

Introduction

A Millenary Tradition of Military Leadership

The history of Vietnam is a long story of struggle for national survival. During the nine centuries of independence, which was wrested from the Chinese in 939 A.D. and lost to the French in 1883, the destiny of this small nation was shaped by two main stresses: resistance to invaders and southward expansion. Because of these stresses, the Vietnamese were able to develop an indomitable national spirit which was manifested in repeated victories against overwhelming invading forces from the North and the conquest of the Khmer and Champa Kingdoms in the South.

This indomitable national spirit crystallized into outstanding traditions of military leadership provided by such venerated national heroes as Tran Hung Dao, Le Loi and Nguyen Hue who saved Vietnam several times from certain defeat and annexation. These traditions came alive again when France conquered Vietnam. Hoang Dieu, the governor of besieged Hanoi, chose suicide rather than surrender. Emperor Ham Nghi joined the armed resistance which continued after his arrest by the French under the leadership of Phan Dinh Phung. From his jungle redoubt of North Vietnam's highlands, Hoang Hoa Tham, the legendary guerrilla chieftain, led a desperate but effective fight against the French colonial government for many years. His arrest and execution in 1913 ended a centuries-old tradition of military leadership which seemed unable to make a resurgence among the nationalists of modern times.

Among the military leaders who had elevated this tradition to its glorious peak, perhaps no one could be the equal of Marshal Tran Hung Dao who twice in 1285 and 1288 soundly defeated the invincible

Golden Horde of Mongolia. The 200,000-man Vietnamese army under his command was certainly no match for the half-million of belligerent Mongol warriors under Thoat Hoan, son of Kublai Khan, who were swarming down the Red River Valley toward Hanoi, the nation's capital. Tran Anh Tong, the humane emperor, was undecided; deep in his heart, he wanted to save his subjects' lives and was inclined to surrender. He confided this idea to his commander-in-chief but Tran Hung Dao urged against such action. When the emperor insisted, Tran Hung Dao imperturbably told him, "If your majesty decides to surrender, you will have to cut off my head first". Inspired by this unflappable will to resist, the national congress, convened by the emperor at the Dien Hong Palace to debate the issue of submission or resistance, unanimously chose to fight. The entire Vietnamese people thus decided to rally behind Tran Hung Dao's leadership and throw itself, body and soul, against the mighty hordes.

But Tran Hung Dao knew he could not defeat the Mongols unless his outnumbered army was imbued with the same determination to fight. To exhort his officers and men and mold them into a cohesive combat force, he circulated the famous "Proclamation" which remains a masterpiece of classic Vietnamese literature. In a paternal and compassionate though sometimes reproachful tone, Tran Hung Dao eloquently spoke of the shame and humiliation of defeat, chided those who neglected their military profession for wordly pleasures, and appealed to all to defend the national honor and restore peace by defeating the Mongols. His words immediately stirred the Vietnamese army into unprecedented action. Officers and men alike vowed to fight to their deaths and all tattooed the words "Sat Dat" (Death to the Mongols) on their forearms as an expression of their determination. And in a succession of brilliant victories, the Vietnamese army stopped the Golden Horde and finally forced it back to China.

This was the most brilliant example of military leadership in the history of Vietnam. Tran Hung Dao indeed knew that he had little chance against such a powerful and gigantic enemy; he also knew that the Vietnamese people and his army were utterly confused and demoralized by rumors about the invincibility of the Mongol Army. Yet Tran Hung Dao resolutely rejected the idea of surrender even though it came from the emperor himself. He skillfully aroused the morale of his troops and people and organized them for counterattack; rare indeed had there been any leader as patriotic and courageous. It was his leadership that inspired the Vietnamese people and army to defeat the oppressors and saved Vietnam again from subjection.

How did Tran Hung Dao manifest his leadership? An analysis of his proclamation will provide us a clue. He began by evoking the ancient heroes' sacrifices as examples for his subordinates to follow. Then he points out the mischievous deeds of the mongols and their incessant demands for tribute which cause him to feel humiliated and outraged; and he vows to avenge the enemy even if it takes his own life. Next, as commander-in-chief, he reminds his men how well he has taken care of them and how together they have shared dangers and glories. He criticizes sharply those who are indifferent or neglect their duties by engaging in games and gambling. He defines the responsibility that every man should take during a national emergency and encourages all of them to devote themselves to studying and practicing the military arts as presented in a manual prepared by himself. Finally, as a reward for success in repulsing the enemy, every man will have his name inscribed in the annals and deserves to be a descendant of our glorious forefathers.

It is obvious that as early as in the 13th century, Tran Hung Dao knew how to apply with skill the following modern principles of leadership:

      Make sound and timely decisions
      Keep your men informed
      Know your men and look out for their welfare
      Set the example
      Develop a sense of responsiblity in your subordinates.

In addition, the dissemination of the proclamation which reads like an important order of the day, was indeed an innovative political warfare technique that few people appreciated at that time.

The Vietnamese people were so grateful to Tran Hung Dao that they elevated him to the rank of a saint after his death and erected many temples dedicated to his cult, especially in North Vietnam. In Saigon, one such temple could be found on Hien Vuong Street where annual rites were performed to commemorate his death. The Vietnamese believed that Tran Hung Dao was created by the "sacred spirit of the country." Born into a royal family, he did not graduate from any military school but studied extensively from ancient manuals on war. He himself prepared a manual on Vietnamese strategy and tactics intended for his officers and men.

Tran Hung Dao was perhaps a born leader. He had all the qualities required of a leader such as behavioral and moral rectitude, courage, initiative, profound knowledge and especially patriotism and loyalty to the emperor. A man who combined talent and ethics such as Tran Hung Dao was unusual indeed. The Mongol invasion made him a "hero of the circumstance". Faced with the danger of foreign domination, he took up his responsibilities and led his army to success.

It was unfortunate that Vietnam did not always have a Tran Hung Dao each time it was threatened by a foreign invasion. This was perhaps one of the many reasons why in the 19th century, France succeeded in taking by force Cochinchina and turned it into a colony by 1862. And despite armed resistance by the loyalists, Annam and Tonkin finally succumbed to French technological superiority in warfare and both became "protectorates" in 1884.

French colonialism, however, aroused an intense awareness of national identity among Vietnamese intellectuals. Beginning with Phan Boi Chau at the turn of the century and culminating in the Viet Minh led uprising in 1945 during which national independence was wrested back for the first time, this awareness produced several nationalist movements and parties whose activities were met with harsh punitive measures by the French. During the ninety years of its rule, the French colonial government imprisoned and executed thousands of Vietnamese patriots, including the famous VNQDD leader, Nguyen Thai Hoc, who were likely to become future leaders. As a foreign observer has aptly described, "By wrecking generation after generation of potential leaders with their thorough repression, they (the French) contributed considerably to Vietnam's present political problems."[1]

Dictated by the constant need to repress indigenous rebellions and political parties, France maintained a sizeable military force in her Indochinese colony. Over the years this force had gone through several reorganizations but remained essentially infantry. There were two categories of infantry. One was regular infantry forces which were responsible for maintaining security throughout Indochina and consisted of from two to three divisions, called Colonial Infantry, made up of French and North African troops such as Senegalese, Moroccans, Tunisians, and Algerians. The Vietnamese called these troops by a derisory term "lính khố đỏ" (the red-loinclothed soldiers) apparently because they all wore a large waistband of red flannel underneath the leather belt. These regular troops were later augmented by French legionnaires. The second category of infantry was the territorial forces, called "Garde Indigène" (Indigenous guard), which were made up mostly of Vietnamese troops under the command of French officers and non-commissioned officers. These forces were assigned guard duties at governmental agencies and public installations such as the governor's office, the courthouse, the treasury, the postal office, water and electricity plants, etc. The strength of the "Garde Indigène" varied according to the importance or the budget of each province. These troops were also called derisively "lính khố xanh" (the blue-loinclothed soldiers) by the Vietnamese.

After several decades of repressive French colonial rule, the Vietnamese people gradually lost their ancient military tradition and were more oriented toward the letters. As a result of this and the anti-French feelings, they always had a very low regard for those Vietnamese who volunteered to serve in the "infanterie coloniale" or

---

[1] Chester A. Bain, <u>Vietnam, The Roots of Conflict</u>, Prentice-Hall, Inc. Englewood Cliffs, New Jersey, 1967, pp. 95-96.

the "garde indigène" whom they contemptuously called "khố xanh, khố đỏ" (bunch of loincloths). Another reason for this low regard was that most of those who enlisted were illiterate or jobless and, because of French policies, they never made it to officer's rank.[2]

Things gradually improved with the advent of World War I during which a number of educated Vietnamese youths volunteered to serve in the French Army as "lính thợ" (specialists). But they were in fact "ouvriers non spécialisés" (non-specialized workers) or laborers and employed as such. Many of them chose to stay behind in France when the war was over. During World War II, France adopted new administrative policies toward Indochina and allowed the selection of Vietnamese youths having a Baccalaureate diploma to be trained as officers. These selected officer-candidates were trained at two special military schools: Tong, in Son Tay Province, North Vietnam, and Thu Dau Mot in South Vietnam. Those candidates who had French nationality (mostly southerners) might be selected to attend the Saint Cyr Military Academy in France. At the same time, a number of Vietnamese career non-commissioned officers with outstanding service records was also selected to attend the Frejus officer school in France. From that time on, the ranks of French colonial infantry in Vietnam were augmented with a number of Vietnamese officers and NCO's.

When Japanese forces overthrew the French colonial government in a lightning military coup on 9 March 1945, a great number of Vietnamese officers and NCO's serving in the French colonial infantry chose to return to civilian life. But some followed their units into China and remained with the French Army. The Japanese occupation did not last long, however; it ended with Japan's surrender in August the same year.

---

[2] The highest rank a few could obtain was "quan" (adjutant or master sergeant). Therefore, quản was regarded as a prestigious rank by the lowly peasants who equated it with quan (mandarin), hence the reverential address "quan quản."

The Viet Minh immediately took advantage of this political vacuum to seize power and establish themselves as the legitimate government of independent Vietnam on 2 September 1945. In the meantime, France was also preparing to reconquer her former colony because, in spite of President Roosevelt's strong opposition, the Allies had agreed to restore French presence in Indochina. With the help of British forces, who had the mission to disarm the defeated Japanese in Indochina south of the 16th parallel, and tacit American approval, the French first retook the southern part of Vietnam by force against heavy resistance by Viet Minh-led guerrillas. But to reconquer the North, they had first to negotiate with the new Vietnamese government under Ho Chi Minh. This government had the blessing of Bao Dai, the former emperor who now served as Supreme Counselor, and enjoyed the support of the Vietnamese people. The weak military posture of Ho Chi Minh's government compelled him to yield to French demands and allow French forces into Hanoi and Hai Phong. But when the French threatened, by ruse and by force, to expand their control from these footholds, the Viet Minh leaders had no choice but to fight. Fighting, in fact, had never ceased since the French returned to Indochina and established its rule in Saigon. But not until France refused to resume negotiations and decided to take over the North by force did Ho Chi Minh resort to armed resistance. On 19 December 1946, he called on the Vietnamese people to attack and oust the French from Hanoi. And thus officially began the First Indochina war.

Birth of the Vietnamese National Army

During the first few years of the war, the French succeeded in occupying most urban areas and key lines of communication. Wherever they established control, they immediately sought collaborators among those Vietnamese who had served under the French colonial regime, such as former mandarins, civil servants, and village officials, to establish a pro-French government. At the same time, they also recruited the veterans of the French colonial infantry and Garde Indigène, assembled them into units, called "forces suppletives" (auxiliary forces) and assigned these units service and support missions.

When the French first set about to reconquer Indochina, they were confident they would succeed with the employment of sheer military force. Politically, therefore, they only sought the collaboration of submissive elements and the local intelligentsia through material rewards. This was typical of French divisive policies which sought to create pro-French political forces and impose colonial rule through these forces. For example, in 1946 the French turned former Cochinchina into a separate state whose government was made up of secessionist, pro-French intellectuals of southern origin. They also transformed the Central Highlands into a French-dominated autonomous state called the Western Dominion and in North Vietnam, they established the autonomous Nung country in the Mong Cay area and the Thai country in the Lai Chau area.

The creation of these autonomous states was immediately followed by the activation of local "forces suppletives." For example, after the government of autonomous Cochinchina was established, the French created the Ve Binh Cong Hoa (Republican Guard) on 1 October 1946, which was subsequently renamed Ve Binh Nam Viet (South Vietnamese Guard). In rapid succession, the French activated the Bao Ve Quan (Protective Forces) which were subsequently redesignated Ve Binh Doan (Guard Corps) in Central Vietnam and the Bao Chinh Doan (Civil Guard) in North Vietnam. All three forces were subsequently called Ve Binh Quoc Gia (National Guard). During the initial stage of their formation, these forces were commanded by French officers of the "Garde Republicaine". Not until 1950 did they begin to receive Vietnamese officers.

During the same period, Vietnamese personnel serving in the French Expeditionary Corps in Indochina could be divided into two categories. The first category consisted of those recruited by French forces either as immediate replacements for French units whose losses could not be replenished entirely by French troops, or to activate new units under French command and control as required by the expanding war. As a result, the French Expeditionary Corps was redesignated "French Union

Forces", a move dictated by political convenience and intended to stimulate the morale of indigenous personnel serving in French units. The French need for additional combat forces led to the creation of these French Union units wherever local manpower was available. Among these units, there were also a few which consisted entirely of ethnic minority groups. Thus, French Union forces included not only Vietnamese units but also Khmer, Montagnard, Nung, Muong and Thai units.

The second category included those Vietnamese serving in separate companies that made up the "forces suppletives." These were units especially created for the maintenance of local security and although under the command of French cadres, they were not part of French Union forces. This was in keeping with French principles of force organization which made a distinction between mobile combat forces and territorial forces. The mobile forces consisted of combat units which were constantly on the move from one combat area to another while territorial forces were made up of administrative and local units responsible for the maintenance of territorial security. These included locally-activated companies of "forces suppletives" belonging to religious sects such as the Hoa Hao, the Cao Dai and the Roman Catholic U.M.D.C.'s.[3]

As the war intensified and after attempts to negotiate with the Viet Minh had failed, France contacted ex-emperor Bao Dai who lived in exile in Hong Kong to put in motion the so-called "nationalist solution." This effort produced the Ha Long Agreement of 5 June 1948 signed by French High Commissioner Emile Bollaert and Bao Dai on the French destroyer, "Duguay Trouin." According to this agreement, France recognized Vietnam as an independent state whose eventual reunification was to be freely accomplished by the Vietnamese themselves. In return, Vietnam declared to join the French Union as an "Associated State."

---

[3] Unités Mobiles de Defense de la Chretiente (Mobile Units for the Defense of Christianity).

As a result of the Ha Long agreement, a provisional central government of Vietnam was established under the premiership of Mr. Nguyen Van Xuan. It was also agreed that French and Vietnamese authorities would cooperate in the organization of various agencies under this government, to include the Vietnamese armed forces. Thus the creation of a Vietnamese National Army was formally decreed by the Ha Long agreement. But this agreement was only a stepping stone toward a formal treaty between France and Vietnam. Not until 8 March 1949 was this treaty finally signed between Bao Dai and the President of the French Republic, Vincent Auriol. By this treaty, France formally recognized Vietnam as an independent and unified nation.

The Vietnamese National Armed Forces, however, were not officially created until a year later, on 11 May 1950. Initial plans called for the activation of a 60,000-man military force, about half of which consisted of regular troops and the other half, of auxiliary troops. The first mission assigned to this national force was to pacify the country and take up part of the combat responsibility heretofore assumed entirely by French forces. During 1950, therefore, several Vietnamese military schools were established, such as the Regional Military Schools, the Junior Military School and the Dalat Inter-Arms Military School. During the initial stage, the commandants, staff officers and instructors of these schools were all French. Only much later were they gradually replaced by Vietnamese officers. In order to provide the necessary cadre for this nascent national army, a great number of Vietnamese officers and NCOs serving in French Union forces were detached to the Vietnamese National Armed Forces. These cadres were subsequently fully integrated into the national forces. Also, a number of auxiliary and French Union units were redesignated and transferred to the national forces even though French officers remained in command. Eventually, these units were all commanded by Vietnamese officers.

Because of the urgent need for Vietnamese leaders at all echelons, training during that period was extensive and accelerated. Vietnamese military schools also received a helping hand from French schools in-country or in France. Many Vietnamese students were selected to attend these schools. Those who qualified for military training in France had to go through an exacting screening procedure and were required to have a good command of French. The training provided by these schools was very comprehensive and usually required more time than in-country training.[4]

During the next few years, the Vietnamese National Armed Forces set about to improve force structure and territorial organization. In May 1951, the Ministry of National Defense began to function officially even though its creation had been sanctioned at the time of the first national government two years earlier. The Ministry of Defense initially assumed the duties of the General Staff which was not created until a year later in May 1952. Then in July 1952, the Vietnamese military regions (MR) were established: the 1st MR encompassed the territory of southern Vietnam, the 2d MR, the territory of central Vietnam, the 3d MR, the territory of northern Vietnam and the 4th MR, the Central Highlands. During the next year, 1953, plans provided for the activation of six mobile infantry groups, each to be made up of three infantry battalions and a number of support units totalling about 4,500 men. These were Mobile Groups Nos. 11, 21, 31, 32, 41 and 42.

The French defeat at Dien Bien Phu on 7 May 1954, however ushered in an emergency situation in northern Vietnam. Desertion was widespread among Vietnamese units, especially of the 3d MR. During the month of May alone, some 4,303 regulars and 694 auxiliary troops became deserters. By the end of May, 1954, the total strength of the Vietnamese Armed Forces stood at 249,517, to include 205,613 regular and 43,904 auxiliary troops. By the time the cease-fire was declared, however, this strength had been substantially depleted by desertion, especially among units located in northern Vietnam. This was a result of deteriorating morale and uncertainty. Under the growing pressure of an enemy on the verge

---

[4] Training in France was suspended in 1955.

of victory, not only had these units been compelled to fight without rest or replacements for long periods of time, they were also critically affected by enemy propaganda and the prospect of having to leave North Vietnam where most of their troops were born.

A French Legacy

Prior to the Geneva Accords of 1954, French forces assumed all responsibilities for combat operations and territorial security in Vietnam despite the existence of the Vietnamese National Armed Forces with their own command and control system. During this period, Vietnamese units operated under the control of French commanders of larger units or territorial commands. Not until much later were a few tactical areas of responsibility placed under Vietnamese authority and this was done only gradually. As a result, the Vietnamese General Staff and military region commands were merely responsible for the organization, administration and training of Vietnamese units.

In brief, it seemed that Vietnam always had to obtain what it wanted the hard way. After World War II, for example, political independence was gained only after tremendous difficulties and several challenges. This was also true for our military forces. Initially, after becoming an "independent state," Vietnam was allowed only a few auxiliary units. Not until the military situation had become difficult with increased losses and slow replacements and not until she was faced with domestic problems did France resort to the "nationalist solution" and think about creating the Vietnamese National Armed Forces. And this did not occur until 4 years after France had returned to Indochina.

The Vietnamese National Armed Forces, therefore, suffered some retardation in their growth, progressing hesitantly from companies to battalions and finally to mobile groups only when the war was about to be concluded. Most Vietnamese battalions were originally those transferred from French Union Forces and their cadres were also those who had served in French units. These Vietnamese officers and NCO's, who did not have the same educational background and uniform military training, differed greatly in command abilities. Vietnamese officers who graduated from Saint Cyr, for example, might have perfect command of French and excellent military knowledge but were qualified only for staff assignments; most of them in fact had very little combat experience. By contrast, the majority of those who graduated from in-country French military schools or came from the enlisted ranks were excellent combatants but bad staff officers. As to those officers who came from auxiliary forces of religious sects, they were usually good in combat but lacked basic military knowledge.

Among the first Vietnamese officers who held important positions, the most notable was perhaps Lieutenant General Nguyen Van Hinh, the first Chief of the General Staff of the Vietnamese National Armed Forces. He was the son of Mr. Nguyen Van Tam, the prime minister. Married to a French woman and of French nationality, General Hinh had served for a long time in the French Air Force. When he came back to Vietnam in 1950, he was a major and assigned the position of secretary general at the Ministry of National Defense. Promoted to lieutenant colonel in 1951, he served as military aide to Chief of State Bao Dai until his appointment as Chief of the General Staff. When Hinh was appointed he was immediately promoted to the rank of Brigadier General. In addition to General Hinh, there were two other officers assigned to key positions. They were Major Tran Van Minh, who was appointed Chief of Staff for General Hinh and Major Tran Van Don, Director of the Military Security Service. Both were of French nationality, graduated from French military schools, and had just completed the command and staff course in Paris.

As part of French Union forces, Vietnamese units also suffered from the same disparity in combat capabilities, primarily because of the purpose for which they were employed and the locality where they were activated. In general, colonial airborne and commando units fought very well while infantry units were rated as only average. As to auxiliary forces and those belonging to religious sects, they were generally poor in combat except for a very few units. During combat operations, which were generally of the mopping-up type, Vietnamese units seldom respected the lives and properties of the local population. Unfortunately, this state of things was remedied only during the last few years of the war.

The training of officers and troops was conducted entirely by French military personnel or at French Union military schools. Training materials, therefore, were all prepared in French and published by the French Ministry of War. Even in Vietnamese military schools, which were commanded and staffed by French officers, French training materials were used and French tactics were taught. Additionally, even though the Vietnamese General Staff was created in 1952, French continued to be used as the official language in the Vietnamese Armed Forces. Not until 1955 was this use terminated and Vietnamese became the official language in all military correspondence.

It is clearly obvious, therefore, that the Vietnamese National Armed Forces were the offspring of the French Union forces whose image they faithfully mirrored and whose flaws and weaknesses they also inherited.

During this period, the basic manual that was most widely referred to and used in Vietnamese military schools besides the training publications disseminated by the French Ministry of War was the "Manuel du Grade" (Manual for Small-Unit Commanders) by Lafargues, published by Lavauzelles. This manual was a compendium of tactics and procedures that army units were required to observe during maneuvers, field bivouacs, garrison, and combat. It also contained lessons in infantry armament, map reading, topography and, in other words, almost everything that a small unit commander had to know to exercise his command. The manual begins with a key statement that thoroughly reflects French military philosophy: "La discipline est la force principale de l'Armée. Les ordres doivent être exécutés sans hésitation, ni murmure" (Discipline is the primary strength of an army. Orders must be carried out without waver or grumble). Emphasis on discipline was thus the mainstay of French forces and this led to a concept of command and leadership based solely on the position and authority of the commander. All subordinates were condemned to be blindfolded executors of any order issued by their superior.

Generations of Vietnamese officers were imbued with this concept of leadership, which they accepted as an indisputable maxim and guidance. Working closely together with and under the tutelage of French cadres for several years, Vietnamese officers were also heavily influenced by the way these French cadres actually exercised command and leadership. They learned certain precepts widely popular in the French officer corps such as:

> "Le sous-lieutenant sait rien, fait rien
> Le lieutenant sait rien, fait tout
> Le capitaine sait tout, fait rien"
>
> (A 2d lieutenant knows nothing, and does nothing
> A 1st lieutenant knows nothing, but does everything
> A captain knows everything, but does nothing)

or

> "Un chef ne fait rien, ne laisse rien faire et fait faire"
> (A leader does not have to do anything, lets nothing disturb him, and makes others work)

or even:

> "Fais ce que je dis mais pas ce que je fais" (Do what I say but not what I do)

Although there is some cynical undertone in these precepts, which at the time were in no way intended as teachings, they nevertheless reveal a certain humorous and pragmatic aspect of some French officers' approach to command and leadership in Vietnam. To the unsophisticated Vietnamese officers who looked up to their French commanders as tutors, these phrases might have been construed as wisdom.

During this period of French tutelage, promotions served as rewards not only for combat exploits but also for loyalty to the French cause. There were many so-called "avancements exceptionnels" (exceptional promotions) awarded solely for political reasons, for example the nomination of Mr. Tran Van Soai alias Năm Lửa, commander of the Hoa Hao auxiliary forces, to the rank of Brigadier General. Perhaps, the French High Command had made this decision to win his loyalty and to exert a certain influence over the Hoa Hao. Thus, in a ceremony held in Cai Von, Colonel Le Nulzec, commander of the Western Zone, solemnly handed to Mr. Tran Van Soai the unusual insignia of brigadier-general with only one star (The French army's insignia of brigadier general had two stars). But subsequently, Mr. Soai was always found wearing a two-star insignia and his uniform was an exact French copy with gold-embroidered kepi. Bay Vien, chief of the Binh Xuyen gang, was also made brigadier general by Chief of State Bao Dai.

One of the questions that should concern students of Vietnamese history was whether or not the Vietnamese National Armed Forces were able to maintain their role and fight with dedication as long as the French still held power? This was precisely the question that concerned the Vietnamese Chief of State, Bao Dai. He did not believe it was possible and confided to a witness:

> "As for me, I have always wished that our nation should have an army of its own. But many people advise me that at the present time we should not develop what we have into a full-fledged army. For it would be detrimental to our nation as long as we cannot provide an ideal for our soldiers to fight for. And as long as these men fight without an ideal, they are apt to desert their ranks in mass and go over to the other side. Tell me, how can we motivate and instill a combat spirit in our soldiers as long as we fail to inspire confidence among our people? We don't have enough command cadres. The army is said to be ours but it is commanded by French officers and employed by the French High Command. If we say that this is our army, then we tacitly admit its mercenary character and how can a mercenary army have any ideal or the support of the population?"[5]

---

[5] The Republic of Vietnam Armed Forces: The Formative Years, 1946-1955, Military History 4, published by J-5/JGS, Military History Division. p. 183.

Thus, the problem that plagued the Vietnamese National Armed Forces from the beginning was the lack of military leaders. It was the legacy we inherited from nearly one century of French domination during which our millenary tradition of military leadership was completely lost. It was a serious problem that South Vietnam was able to solve only belatedly although beginning in 1954 all of our units were commanded by Vietnamese officers. But even then, national authority was still largely in the hands of the French who made all the decisions concerning the conduct of the war and politics, this despite the fact that some areas had been placed under Vietnamese military control. This situation was not resolved until the advent of the 1954 Geneva Accords and Mr. Ngo Dinh Diem became prime minister. And only then did Vietnam enjoy genuine independence, complete sovereignty and an independent army.

Such was the status of military leadership in the Vietnamese National Armed Forces at the eve of Vietnam's partition and before South Vietnam even became a new nation south of the 17th parallel.

In order to have a frame of reference for my discussions on leadership as it was practiced in the Republic of Vietnam Armed Forces, I think it necessary to review briefly how leadership is being conceived and applied in more advanced countries.

By contrast to previous centuries during which the weaponry used to make war was still rudimentary and man was still basically simple, the advent of scientific inventions, modern technology and industry during the 20th century have made war more sophisticated and devastating. Man has also acquired more knowledge, does more thinking and lives under the heavy influence of social and scientific progress. As a problem, leadership has therefore become more complex and to be a good leader, one has to be many things. As an example, a good leader is required to:

"Study human behavior which will help him (the leader) to acquire the knowledge required to understand himself and his men, to learn why men act and react in certain ways, to identify various types of behavior, and to learn how to influence the behavior of subordinates so that their personal goals complement or reinforce the unit's goal. In addition, the study of human behavior will give the leader the knowledge with which to apply the principles of leadership effectively."[6]

"The principles have stood the test of time and have guided the conduct and action of successful leaders of the past. Throughout history, these have, in varying degrees, influenced the actions of every successful leader. The fact that every leader has not always made full use of each one of these principles does not make them any less valid. Although their application may vary with the situation, a leader who disregards them risks failure. These guidelines are the principles of leadership:

1. Know yourself and seek self-improvement
2. Be technically and tactically proficient
3. Seek responsibility and take responsibility for your actions
4. Make sound and timely decisions
5. Set the example
6. Know your men and look out for their welfare
7. Keep your men informed
8. Develop a sense of responsibility in your subordinate
9. Insure that the task is understood, supervised, and accomplished
10. Train your men as a team
11. Employ your unit in accordance with its capabilities.[7]

If we accept these guidelines as true and universal for every modern army, then "leadership that is based primarily on position and authority and is lacking empathy will, in the long run, prove ineffective."[8] This ineffectiveness in leadership was also a major problem

---

[6] FM 22-100, Military Leadership, Hq., Department of the Army; June 1973, p. 5-1.

[7] Ibid., p. 2-6.

[8] Ibid., p. 2-6.

that plagued the Vietnamese Armed Forces during their formative years under French tutelage and influence. One may say that during this period there were only commanders and no leaders because all of them seemed to mimic French officers whose concept of leadership, as has been explained, derived primarily from position and authority.

What then makes a successful, effective leader besides these guidelines?

"When a study of the personalities of a group of successful leaders was conducted, fourteen traits were identified as common to the group. Possession of these traits by itself does not guarantee success but apparently, they are most desirable in all leaders. The traits are:

Bearing, courage (moral and physical), decisiveness, dependability, endurance, enthusiasm, initiative, integrity, judgement, justice, knowledge, loyalty, tact, unselfishness."[9]

These traits and principles of leadership will serve as a frame of reference for the discussions that follow in the next three chapters on examples illustrative of Vietnamese military leadership at all levels of command during the various periods of the Vietnam war.

---

[9] Ibid., p. 2-1.

CHAPTER II

Leadership Under President Diem's Regime

Background

On 16 June 1954, Chief of State Bao Dai designated Mr. Ngo Dinh Diem, then living in exile in the U.S., as prime minister after promising him considerable authority in political and military affairs. However, within just a few weeks after he took office on 7 July 1954, Prime Minister Diem realized that he actually had no authority at all. Power in the State of Vietnam remained fractured, as in the past; portions were held by a number of fiercely competing factions. The interests of the groups among whom it was divided were quite compatible with those of the French, whose domination had rested largely on the ancient principle of "divide and rule". In addition, to dealing with the chaotic political conditions he inherited from the colonial regime, Diem faced equally discouraging tasks on several other fronts. The country was in ruins. Most bridges had been blown up. Canals, roads, railways, telephone and telegraph services had been either destroyed or were in disrepair; vast regions of rice land were uncultivated; countless peasants who had fled the countryside found themselves unemployed in the cities. And Diem's administration, run by an incompetent civil service, politically hostile and disintegrating, had to provide the human and material resources for receiving, feeding, and temporarily settling hundreds of thousands of refugees who had fled from the North to the South, adding enormous burdens to a totally insolvent state and government. With his aspiration to give the country a unified and strong government, Diem represented the supreme national needs of the hour. But how could he overcome the obstructions of the many forces and factions hostile or indifferent to his efforts? He was opposed by the army, which was still under French command and headed by Vietnamese officers appointed by Bao Dai and the French. He was disobeyed by the police and the secret service, which Bao Dai had sold to the Binh Xuyen, his closest ally among the sects. Diem's national aims clashed with the "feudal" power structures of the Hoa Hao and Cao Dai sects, which with their private armies ruled most of the country west and south of Saigon. He met the hostility of the French and Chinese circles who controlled much of the Vietnamese economy and who knew that a strong national regime was bound to limit their powers. This was true also for the Vietnamese landlords, who feared that Diem's call for national "revolution" implied radical projects of agrarian reform. The old collaborators inside and outside the administration sabotaged Diem's every step to secure control of the existing government apparatus, and the old "fence-sitters", the attentists, now more numerous than ever among the intellectuals, refused to support Diem out of fear of an early collapse of his regime and a take-over of the South by the Viet Minh. This possible take-over was indeed the greatest of all dangers that threatened Diem, and together with everything else was the reason that the chances for the survival of Diem's regime were generally regarded as nil.[1]

This was how bleak the situation of South Vietnam looked when Ngo Dinh Diem took office. In the contemporary history of Vietnam, perhaps Mr. Diem was the only leader to be confronted with the partition of the country as soon as he was appointed and the numerous, difficult problems involved that he had to solve.

The Diem administration placed first priority on negotiations with the French for the immediate transfer of military and administrative authorities to the government of South Vietnam. The French agreed only to a gradual transfer. On 27 September, 1954, however, an agreement was reached in Washington between the United States and France whereby

---

[1] Joseph Buttinger, <u>Vietnam: A Dragon Embattled</u>, Frederick A. Praeger, New York, 1967, pp. 852-853.

all military, economic, financial and commercial powers that France still held would be transferred to the government of South Vietnam beginning on 1 January 1955. By this agreement, the United States also agreed to provide aid directly to the independent nation of South Vietnam, and the French Expeditionary Corps would be repatriated upon request of the South Vietnamese government. In reality, French forces redeployed from the Saigon-Cholon area to Vung Tau on 20 May 1955 and withdrew completely from South Vietnam only on 28 April 1956.

In early September 1954, the chief of the Vietnamese General Staff, Lt. Gen. Nguyen Van Hinh, openly attacked Prime Minister Diem, who responded by ordering him on a mission to France for six months. General Hinh resisted Diem's orders, arguing that since Chief of State Bao Dai appointed him to his present position, only the Chief of State could remove him from office. The conflict dragged on for three tense months, creating confusion and divisions within the armed forces. Although General Hinh was in control of the armed forces, he did not dare use force to overthrow Prime Minister Diem, fully aware that Mr. Diem had strong American support. Several army units, repulsed by General Hinh's rebellious and pro-French attitude, manifested their support for the prime minister. Most remarkable was the action taken by Major Thai Quang Hoang (later promoted to lieutenant general) who as commander of the Ninh Thuan sector, took to the maquis with 700 of his men in a rebellion against the General Staff. His action was supported by several other units located in the Phan Thiet and Nha Trang areas. Fearing an army-wide rebellion, finally Chief of State Bao Dai summoned General Hinh to France and subsequently removed him from office on 29 November 1954. Prime Minister Diem immediately appointed Brigadier General Le Van Ty, then commander of the 1st Military Region, to replace General Hinh as Chief of the General Staff.

The Diem government thus survived the first momentous challenge and endeavored to eliminate the remaining obstacles on its way toward national unity and stability. In early 1955, the National Bank of Vietnam was created to receive American aid funds and began issuing Vietnamese banknotes and coins. As of that time, the Vietnamese monetary system became independent and entirely disassociated from the Bank of Indochina and the franc zone of influence.

The Vietnamese National Armed Forces, meanwhile, activated four infantry divisions on 1 January, 1955; these were the 6th (Nung) Division, 11th, 21st and 31st Divisions. But in contrast to previous years, the General Staff had to interrupt this development trend because of a force structure ceiling imposed by the U.S. Military Assistance Advisory Group (MAAG). The decision to cut back on military assistance came as a surprise for the General Staff, which was informed only at the end of 1954. In early 1955, therefore, the General Staff took emergency measures to bring the total strength down to the imposed ceiling within the prescribed time. At that time, MAAG desired to reduce the total strength by one half, from over 200,000 to 100,000. In MAAG's view, the Vietnamese Armed Forces having no longer to fight a war should be reorganized and trimmed down to perform a peace time mission. In addition, MAAG also advised the General Staff against maintaining a professional army composed entirely of volunteers. Instead, the Vietnamese Army should include a draft component and rotate this component in and out of service every 18 months, the legal duration of military services for conscripts. After the 18 months of mandatory service, the draftees would be discharged and become reservists "on call." In brief, the MAAG-conceived force structure plan was designed to maintain an adequate defense force at all times without having to incur big expenditures. The Vietnamese General Staff, meanwhile, suggested that a force structure of 150,000 be maintained, which, it argued, was not in violation of the Geneva Accords and would provide for the effective defense of the national territory. But this recommendation was rejected by MAAG and as a result, the Vietnamese General Staff was compelled to implement a large-scale discharge program without being prepared for it. The sudden and arbitrary discharge of thousands of NCO's and enlisted men created an emotional shock throughout the ranks. It also provoked two mass demonstrations staged by disabled veterans, one in Hue and one in Nha Trang, in which the discharged servicemen raised protests against the government's action and demanded compensations and jobs. Units also met with difficulties when servicemen who had been retained beyond the terms of their contracts and NCOs with large families refused to leave their organizations.

Plans for the discharge called for disbanding all auxiliary force units, estimated at over 33,000 men, releasing about 30,000 "unserviceable" servicemen (to include 8,000 disabled) and removing about 5,000 servicemen with tainted records. This was accomplished during the month of January 1955. The next step involved the mass discharge of all reserve and active duty servicemen falling into these categories: over-aged, retained in service beyond contract terms, draftees having served more than two years, and volunteers having more than two years of service and willing to cancel their contracts. The total of these discharges, which were accomplished during the month of March 1955, amounted to between 43,000 and 50,000.

In addition to problems of discharge, the General Staff was also faced with insistent requests from the French High Command to accept the transfer of about 25,000 French Union troops. In view of the difficulties caused by the 100,000 ceiling, the General Staff was able to accept only 10,000 men, mostly combat-experienced troops and specialists, to include 1,200 paratroopers and 3,000 command auxiliaries.[2] The remaining French Union troops who were not accepted were disbanded. However, an estimated 5,000 to 8,000 of them managed to follow French forces into Algeria.

To solve the economic and social problems caused by the mandatory discharge and also to win over these veterans, the Diem government created the Civil Guard on 8 April 1955, which was supported by the national budget and placed under the control of the Ministry of Interior. In mid-June 1955, when MAAG approved the 150,000-force structure plan, the General Staff suspended discharge orders. By that time, however, 58,445 servicemen had already been removed from military payrolls

---

[2] These commando auxiliaries formed the nuclei of marine units to be subsequently activated.

and the strength of the Vietnamese National Armed Forces stood at 167,555.

A prominent Vietnamese historian commented on the mass discharge of 1955 as follows:

> "The general consensus was that the mass discharge of 1955 was an act which was both psychologically destructive and detrimental to the combat potential of the armed forces. At least 6,000 experienced NCOs who made up the combat elite of the army and the nuclei of several units had been unfortunately released from service. The result was evident. By early 1960 when the Viet Minh resumed their war activities, several of our combat units suffered from ineffectiveness because instead of dedicated and combat-experienced NCOs, they only had green draftees who were not only inexperienced but also weak and cowardly. The government tried to make amends by reinstating these discharged NCOs but only a few were willing to come back. Most of them had either been settled in their civilian jobs or refused to respond because they were still disenchanted by the government's treatment."[3]

With the new 150,000 force structure, the General Staff planned to have a combat force composed of:

- 4 field divisions
- 6 light divisions
- 1 airborne brigade
- 4 armored cavalry regiments
- 11 artillery battalions
- 13 territorial regiments
- 6 infantry regiments of religious troops

In addition, it also set about reinforcing and improving central and regional agencies. And except for minor modifications, this force structure plan remained unchanged until 1964.

---

[3] *The Republic of Vietnam Armed Forces, Formative Years: 1946-1955*, Military History Division, J-5, JGS, Saigon, p. 251.

On 23 October 1955, a nation-wide referendum was held on the issue of whether or not to maintain Bao Dai as Chief of State. An overwhelming majority (98.2%) of the population voted for his dismissal and expressed confidence in the leadership of Prime Minister Diem. Three days later, on 26 October 1955, Diem became President of the Republic of Vietnam, and the National Armed Forces were redesignated the Republic of Vietnam Armed Forces (RVNAF). President Diem also decreed that the day he took office was to become the National Day.

Looking back on the first eighteen months of his administration, no one could dispute the fact that President Diem had achieved many important things and overcome seemingly insurmountable obstacles. The difficulties which he had been required to face were so immense, so numerous that several foreign observers did not think his regime could survive beyond one year. But not only did it survive, he regained complete sovereignty for the new nation, administratively, diplomatically, and militarily. He skillfully maneuvered the withdrawal of the French Expeditionary Corps from South Vietnam, imparted unity and loyalty to the armed forces, and eliminated all armed religious sects that had imposed their control over several areas. At the same time, he effectively reorganized the nation's administrative and military apparatus and most importantly, he laid the foundation for a political regime which could confront and compete with the communist state of North Vietnam and ensure for South Vietnam a position of its own in international affairs. Several people who had criticized him now reversed themselves and heaped praise on him, the man they credited with bringing about a "miracle."

During the following years, under President Diem's leadership, South Vietnam confidently tread its way toward progress and prosperity. The entire monetary system underwent reorganization as did budgetary affairs and central banking. There was a dramatic increase in the number of hospitals, dispensaries, maternity clinics, and public health facilities. Progress in the field of education was equally remarkable. During a four-year period, from 1955 to 1959, the number of students attending community elementary schools increased almost

threefold. Nearly 10,000 students were enrolled in universities by
the end of that period, including about 2,000 who studied abroad. To
provide an efficient bureaucracy for his administration, President Diem
enlarged the National Institute of Administration which not only trained
future civil servants but also provided career improvement courses in
law and economics.

Sustained by political stability and relative peace, the national
economy gradually recovered. In agriculture, rice production which
stood at 2.6 million metric tons in 1954, rose to 3.4 million in 1956
and 5 million in 1959. Progress in the production of rubber was even
greater, topping prewar levels in 1955. The prewar levels were also
reached a few years later in the production of coffee and by the
fishing industry while production figures of all other agricultural
crops although rising considerably still remained below prewar levels.

Industrialization was also a significant effort undertaken by
the Diem government. Major projects included the extensive exploitation
of the Nong Son coal mine, the nation's only one, the construction of
the Da Nhim hydroelectric plant and irrigation dam with Japanese war
reparation payments, the Bien Hoa industrial zone, and the Ha Tien
cement plant.

To help boost economic development and regulate population density,
President Diem instituted the national policy of pioneer farming, which
capitalized on the establishment of agrovilles in uncultivated areas.
A special agency, called the General Commission of Pioneer Farming,
was created in 1957 to implement various plans aimed at resettling about
50,000 peasants from the aridlands of Central Vietnam to the fertile
Central Highlands. This agency employed hundreds of engineers and
technicians for the study of soils and the different crops to be planted
in each area. It also procured and maintained bulldozers, tilling machines, and pumps and developed farming projects for the settlers. In
addition to its economic and demographic purposes, the pioneer farming
program also sought to achieve a strategic objective: regaining complete control over areas, usually remote, that the Viet Minh had used
as sanctuaries. By 1958, another program was initiated—the "agroville"

program—which sought to establish farming communities where population was sparse and scattered. Several such agrovilles had taken shape in the Mekong Delta and elsewhere when Communist insurgent activities began to increase. Because of their vulnerability to Communist attacks, the agrovilles gradually gave way to strategic hamlets which were formally initiated in early 1962. All three programs, despite different names, approaches and techniques, sought to achieve a common objective: to provide security and livelihood for the peasantry and increase production. Unfortunately the success of these programs was hindered in some areas by the poor performance of officials involved.

Politically, the Diem government endeavored to strengthen the democratic base of the regime by instituting general elections. Three such elections were organized in 1956, 1959 and 1963 to elect members of the National Assembly and one in 1961 to reelect the president. To further strengthen the regime and compete politically with North Vietnam, several political organizations were created such as the National Revolution Movement, the National Movement of Revolutionary Civil Servants, the Republican Youth, and most notoriously, the Personalist Labor Party (Dang Can Lao Nhan Vi) conceived as a political opponent to the Communist Party of North Vietnam. The party chairman was Ngo Dinh Nhu, the President's younger brother, who was also credited with formulating the doctrine of personalism as an ideological antithesis to Communism. Graduated from the Ecole des Chartres de Paris, Mr. Nhu was a meditative, severe scholar reputed for his intellectual brilliance. Serving as political counselor for President Diem, Mr. Nhu was not unlike the "eminence grise" of the regime. Apparently an adaptation of Emmanuel Mounier's personalism, Mr. Nhu's doctrinal version or "Nhan Vi," while admitting its Christian inspiration, claimed independence from Christianity. It purported to point a way, the way of duty and true liberty through which a person could liberate himself from capitalism and Marxism by his participation in the life of social groups—family, church, trade unions, etc. "Personalism," it was claimed, did not set out to be a hard and fast system of ideas, but a succession of intuitions marking a road each must follow on his own and as far as he can.[4] To another author, personalism "is a compromise between Marxist collectivism and Western individualistic capitalism while stressing Vietnamese values."[5]

Adopting Communist techniques of organization, the Personalist Labor Party kept its activities underground and never held open meetings or even had an official spokesman. Party members were selected among those loyal to the regime and having a long record of struggling for it. They were also mostly officials who held key positions in the political, administrative and military organizations of the nation.

In the RVNAF, the incorporation of the Personalist Labor Party system within their ranks initially caused some resentment and friction among officers. There were several cases in which NCO's overruled or infringed on the authority of unit commanders simply because they were high-ranking party members. In time, however, these irregularities ceased to exist and most key military commanders eventually became high-ranking party members. There still existed non-members who held key command positions but those were the exceptions who had fully proved their ability and talent.

As to the civilian government and private sector, most agencies and organizations were dominated or led by party members who also controlled the National Revolution Movement and the National Revolution Movement of Revolutionary Civil Servants. Since all civil servants in the central and local bureaucracies were enrolled in the latter movement, they were naturally under the control of the party. Activities of both movements included conducting meetings to denounce Communism, participating in pro-government demonstrations or big ceremonies and voting for government-designated candidates in elections.

---

[4] Dennis J. Duncanson, Government and Revolution in Vietnam, Oxford University Press, London, 1968, p. 216.

[5] Vietnam, The Roots of Conflict, op. cit., p. 118.

Returning from the U.S. Army Command and General Staff College in the summer of 1957, I had the privilege to begin a close professional association with President Diem that lasted for nearly three years. I was assigned to the Presidential Palace as the President's Chief of Staff. He looked to me for military advice and all orders he had for the Joint General Staff he gave to me for transmittal. I saw first hand the strong talent for leadership President Diem exhibited, his great concern for the people of Vietnam, and the earnest efforts he made on behalf of security for the country.

I also came to appreciate the brilliance of Mr. Nhu, the President's brother. He was an innovative thinker—not a real leader as was Diem— but a man of ideas. The President would sign no paper or utter any prepared speech unless Mr. Nhu had first reviewed and approved it. Indeed, Mr. Nhu personally wrote most of Diem's speeches and was responsible for developing all major aspects of national policy and strategy during this period.

While the Diem government devoted its efforts to nation-building, North Vietnam began to initiate disruptive activities following President Diem's rejection of elections toward unification. Former Viet Minh cadres who remained in South Vietnam after 1954 were ordered into action. At the same time, North Vietnam reinfiltrated in the South those cadres who had regrouped to the North. The insurgency thus began and gradually picked up in scope and intensity. From sabotage and assassination, terrorist actions stepped up into small-scale attacks against remote outposts and finally developed into battalion-size warfare. On 26 January 1960, the first of such attacks was conducted against the rear base of the 12th Light Division in Trang Sup, Tay Ninh Province. The defenders were caught unprepared because most personnel of the rear base were attending a Tet party. The Communists succeeded in seizing a large quantity of weapons, clothing and materiel. Lieutenant Colonel Tran Thanh Chieu, the division commander, was immediately removed after this unfortunate event.

To counter the communist insurgency, President Diem created the Ranger Forces whose concept took after the French Commandos of the 1949-1954 war. His plans initially met with opposition from MAAG, which not only suspected a political motive, but objected to the transferring of the most experienced officers' and men from established units to the Rangers. In the face of growing insurgency, however, MAAG finally agreed to support the Ranger forces by providing Special Forces teams to train them. When they were activated, the Vietnamese Ranger forces numbered about 9,000 men, or 65 companies, originally transferred from infantry battalions on the basis of one rifle company per battalion (each battalion had then 4 rifle companies). Later these companies were increased to 86. A Ranger Training Center was also established at Duc My at the old Command School. With the support of U.S. Special Forces this center was well equipped and organized to conduct courses in jungle and swamp combat. Each Ranger course initially lasted three weeks but was subsequently increased to five weeks. Beginning in 1961, MAAG also agreed to increase the RVNAF force structure from 150,000 to 170,000.

Despite President Diem's leadership and his many accomplishments —or, perhaps in some cases because of them—he had many enemies within the country besides the Communists. And despite his brilliance, Mr. Nhu took too little account of the public's animosity toward him as the President's counselor, animosities that were naturally transferred to the president himself. Reflecting the political turmoil that still weakened the country, even though remarkable progress had been made in virtually all aspects of national life, opponents of the regime, not content to follow constitutional processes, plotted violent means to supplant the elected leadership of the country. One attempt took place in November 1960 in which Colonel Nguyen Chanh Thi employed his paratroopers to initiate the coup which ultimately ended in failure. The second attempt took place in February 1962 when two dissident pilots bombed the Independence Palace with their A-1 Skyraiders. This attack caused considerable damage to the old palace which was later rebuilt. But in 1963 a new group of plotters exploited the riotous situation caused by the dissident Buddhists and gathered enough strength, and American support, to depose the Diem government.

The self-immolation of Reverend Thich Quang Duc and other monks effectively burned the bridge of possible reconciliation between the

Diem government and the Buddhists. Mrs. Ngo Dinh Nhu, who derided the Buddhist self-immolation as "a barbecue party", joined her husband in demanding that the Buddhist protesters be crushed, charging that they were communist-led extremists. The U.S., meanwhile, urged the government to make concessions and exile the Nhus. This was a completely impractical idea. It was no more possible for President Diem to banish his brother that to sever his own head. Mr. Nhu was not only the President's brains, he was his most loyal and trusted adviser and supporter.

While President Diem was still undecided, on August 21, elements of the Vietnamese Special Forces attacked the Xa Loi and other pagodas in Saigon, apparently under Mr. Nhu's orders. The monks and even the nuns were brutally beaten and apprehended. Thousands of students and teachers who demonstrated for the monks were arrested and all high schools and universities were ordered closed. This heavy-handed repression enraged many officials, military officers and professionals whose children were manhandled and jailed. It also ended support for the Diem regime at home and abroad.

The U.S. seemed to have rushed the unraveling of events by suspending subsidies for imports and support for the Special Forces. Enraged, Nhu acrimoniously accused Americans and other foreign elements of plotting against the Diem government. Encouraged by the American attitude, several army officers began to plot Diem's overthrow. One group was led by Colonel Do Mau, the trusted director of the Military Security Service, and Major General Tran Thien Khiem, Chief of Staff of the JGS. Do Mau and Khiem were joined by other officers, students and workers. Another group which included Generals Tran Van Don, Duong Van Minh, and Le Van Kim, enlisted the cooperation of Lt. Gen. Do Cao Tri, commander of I Corps and Lt. Gen. Nguyen Khanh, commander of II Corps.

Ngo Dinh Nhu knew that the generals were plotting against him and Diem, but, lacking the evidence, he could not crack down on them. Using a machiavellian scheme, he feigned collusion with Ton That Dinh, the III Corps Commander and Diem's most trusted general, and plotted to seize leadership from Diem. He was hoping that Dinh, whom he suspected as a plotter, would give away the co-conspiring generals. But Nhu's scheme worked against him when Dinh, who had been won over by Do Mau, decided to join forces with the generals.

And so the conspiracy went undetected until the generals decided to strike. On 1 November government troops entered Saigon and seized control. Within hours, the president and his brother were both brutally murdered. The First Republic was over and Vietnam had lost a great leader.

Training and Leadership Development in the RVNAF

To assist with the development of the Vietnamese Armed Forces, the Training Relations Instruction Mission (TRIM) was established in early February 1955 with the objective to study and develop training programs and provide training aids for the Vietnamese military and service schools. The newly developed programs placed emphasis on two areas: (1) recruit training and individual and unit refresher training; (2) unit training and field exercises for major units.

At the same time, the General Staff felt it necessary to reorganize the entire training base for quick adaptation to the new training system and techniques. As the first step, all recruit training centers scattered throughout the country were deactivated and consolidated into a single training center, Training Center No. 1 (later redesignated Quang Trung). Training Center No. 1 conducted not only basic training for all recruits and draftees but also refresher courses for individuals and units. Another effort was expended to consolidate all army service schools into a single facility at the Thu Duc School complex which still included the Reserve Officers School. This consolidation effort also saw the disbandment of all regional military schools and training centers whose responsibilities were now assumed by two institutions: the NCO Academy at Nha Trang and the Inter-Service Military School at Dalat for the training of NCO's and officers respectively.

A new draft policy which differed radically from the mobilization policy instituted in 1950 was implemented soon after the cease-fire. This new policy called into mandatory service only those youths between 20 and 22 years of age to the exclusion of all other ages. The Diem government considered this military obligation a sacred mission that every youth of that age had to carry out. To encourage popular response to the draft, the government initiated a country-wide emulation program for the provinces which culminated in elaborate ceremonies to send the draftees off. When they arrived at processing centers, these draftees were also welcomed at reception parties like honored guests. Training Center No. 1, which had been selected as the main training facility for the draftees, was greatly enlarged to accommodate the increasing numbers of trainees. It was in fact the combination of three former military schools: Trung Chanh, Cay Diem, and Quan Tre.

In addition to training new recruits, Training Center No. 1 also conducted command and leadership courses. Begun in June 1955, these courses were designed to teach U.S. Army tactics and military techniques to Vietnamese officers and NCO's who, while as students, were not allowed to wear rank insignia. Each course lasted three weeks and was devoted to such subjects as basic drill, combat tactics and marksmanship as taught in U.S. service schools. In particular, the students found this new type of training more demanding physically and its methods more elaborate than in French Schools. They also had to submit to an unusually rigorous discipline which along with hard training constituted the basic ingredients of the American way of developing good combat soldiers. The command and leadership course was subsequently redesignated a refresher course for officers and NCO's and its duration increased from three to six weeks. After 24 such courses, training responsibility was reassigned to division commanders. As a direct result of this newly assigned mission, each infantry division began to establish a training center of its own.

The impact of the command and leadership course was far reaching and extremely beneficial to the Vietnamese National Army, whose outlook as a modern military force began to take shape almost immediately. Only a short time following the first few courses, the bearing and appearance of Vietnamese servicemen seemed to change completely. At the General Staff, for example, officers and NCO's were seen neat and elegant in their well-pressed starched khaki uniforms, close crew cuts, and shining black regulation shoes, going about their duties with correct deportment and a disciplined manner. The same was true with field units, the majority of whose personnel displayed the same commendable deportment and manner and were equally smart in their new combat fatigues and boots.

Unit training was the responsibility of unit commanders. The training cycle for an infantry division was 25 weeks allocated as follows:

Preliminary refresher training:	8 weeks
Basic unit training (Company):	7 weeks
Advanced unit training (Battalion):	3 weeks
Advanced unit training (Regiment):	3 weeks
Division exercises:	4 weeks

During the first phase of unit training, which terminated at the battalion level, particular emphasis was placed on marksmanship and movement on foot. Marksmanship training was greatly facilitated by the profuse availability of training ammunition. All units were required to practice movement on foot, by day and by night, over increasing distances up to 30 kms and over all types of terrain. Each soldier was to carry a backpack load from 12 to 15 kilos while participating in these exercises. It was felt that this kind of training would greatly enhance the physical endurance and agility of the individual soldier in real combat situations. Unit training at the regimental level was marked only by staff exercises at headquarters. The final phase of unit training, which involved the entire division as a unit, included both command post exercises and field maneuvers. The training process at divisions continued at an enthusiastic and busy pace until 1959 when it was suspended altogether because of combat operations required to counter increased insurgent activities.

In conjunction with the reorganization of training centers and military schools and the improvement of the training base, training aids and materials also became Americanized because of their increased availability and use within the Vietnamese Army. A training film and equipment exchange was established on 1 October 1955 with a well-stocked film library and 16-mm movie projectors. Vugraphs and vugraph illustration kits were also distributed to units on a loan basis along with 35-mm slide projectors. The General Staff Training Bureau (later to become Central Training Command) also received increasing numbers of graphic training aids which were distributed to units. The translation of U.S. training films into Vietnamese was performed by the Training Aid Section of TRIM. These translations were recorded on tapes and replayed on tape recorders in synchronization with film projections. As to training materials, over 20,000 U.S. military publications were received by TRIM during 1955 alone. These publications were distributed to U.S. advisers and Vietnamese units for their use in conducting training. To further assist training centers and military schools, large working models depicting the parts and actions of rifles, carbines, machine-guns and compasses were also made available by TRIM along with models of rifle sighting devices.

To provide instructors for military schools, a large number of company-grade officers was selected to attend the U.S. Army Infantry School at Fort Benning, Georgia and other service schools beginning in September 1955. A few field-grade officers were also sent to Fort Leavenworth, Kansas, as early as June 1955. In addition to training at U.S. Army service schools, Vietnamese officers also made U.S. sponsored orientation tours to South Korea and the Philippines where they observed modern training facilities and techniques. During the first fiscal year of this overseas training process, as many as 3,644 Vietnamese officers and enlisted men were trained under the Off-shore School Program in the continental U.S. installations and schools and 726 were trained at overseas U.S. Army installations.[6]

Vietnamese career officers received training at the Dalat Military Academy beginning with the 3d class, (the 1st and 2d classes were trained in Hue). The selection of cadets for the Dalat Military Schools was

---

[6] BG James L. Collins, Jr., The Development and Training of the South Vietnamese Army, 1950-1972, DA: Washington, D.C., 1975, p. 15.

careful and highly competitive. Candidates were required to be physically qualified, single, and between the ages of 18 and 22. Except for those who had already earned a baccalaureate diploma, candidates had to compete in an entrance examination and on the average, out of 10 candidates, only two or three were accepted. The duration of training was initially 12 months; it was subsequently increased to two years in 1956 and four years in 1966.

Draftees who had the baccalaureate or a higher diploma were selected to attend the Reserve Officer School at Thu Duc to become reserve officers. The duration of their training as officers was only nine months.

As to non-commissioned officers, whether career or reserve, they were all trained at the NCO Academy at Nha Trang. To be admitted as NCO Cadets, candidates were required to have the junior high school diploma.

The training program for NCO's was eighteen weeks. The first nine weeks or phase one were devoted to the same basic and refresher individual training every recruit was required to undergo. The second phase, also nine weeks, trained the soldiers to be a leader capable of commanding an infantry squad. Upon graduation, the students received the rank of sergeant. Beginning in 1970, however, following a move to unify training, the NCO Academy no longer conducted basic training or the first phase and was entirely devoted to the training of squad leaders. As a result, NCO candidates were trained at the nearest National Training Center for the first phase which was called "preparatory NCO course." Only when they graduated from this course were the trainees sent to the NCO Academy for the second phase or NCO training. As of 1966, the NCO Academy at Nha Trang also conducted special NCO courses for those enlisted men who qualified on the basis of their combat performance but did not have the required junior high school diploma.

The selection of officers and NCO's for the Vietnamese National Army was thus almost entirely based on academic achievements or formal education. Some criticism arose that the armed forces were under the control of the educated urbanites—the rich people—and that such selection lacked a popular base. This criticism was partly true, especially during the formative years of the Vietnamese Armed Forces. Perhaps during that period, academic background was the only criterion available for selective purposes. During the following years, as South Vietnam developed, the educational base was greatly enlarged with the proliferation of schools at all levels to include higher education, and the number of students with academic achievements also increased manyfold and represented a wide cross-section of society. Thus, although education was still the criterion for selections, such criticism no longer held true as far as the lack of popular base was concerned.

In summary, by the end of 1955, the Vietnamese National Armed Forces still maintained the following military schools and training centers:

> The Command and Staff College
>
> The Dalat Military Academy
>
> The Thu Duc Reserve Officer's School
>
> The Medical College (later changed into the Medical Training Center)
>
> The Commando and Physical Education School (later transformed into the NCO Academy)
>
> The Junior Military School
>
> Training Centers Nos. 1 and 4
>
> The Driver and Mechanic Training Center
>
> The Signal Training Centers Nos. 1 and 2
>
> The Military Intelligence and Psywar School

In terms of command and control, a major aspect of Vietnamese military organization that gave rise to shortcomings and problems was the existence of dual channels at the top level. When the Vietnamese Armed Forces began to take shape, it was the Ministry of Defense, which initially exercised command and control, being activated first. For a short time, therefore, this ministry performed the functions of a General Staff, which was not created until late 1951. Perhaps as a result of this, certain control channels continued to emanate from the Secretary of State for Defense, especially in the areas of intelligence, personnel, psywar and inspections, bypassing the Chief of the General

Staff entirely.[7] All procurement, accounting, and budgeting, and the management of military properties were also under the control of the Ministry of Defense. This was a key feature of the Vietnamese defense structure in which the President of the Republic was also Minister of Defense, assisted by a Secretary of State for defense. *(Chart 1)* As a result, the Chief of the General Staff, the military region commanders and the division commanders were required to report directly to the President for important matters or at his summons. A special radio network installed at the presidential palace provided the President with direct communications with corps and division commanders from whom he obtained reports and to whom he often gave orders.

The promotion of officers was a responsibility of the Personnel Directorate operating directly under the Secretary of State for Defense. Every year, this directorate compiled a list of promotion candidates, usually kept strictly confidential, and submitted it to the President for decision. When he reviewed this list, the President usually consulted the Director of Military Security or other heads of agencies as required, but he himself decided who should be promoted. Therefore, promotion during those years was highly selective and difficult. The same procedure applied to the appointment of military officers in key positions; it was all decided by the President.

The Military Assistance Advisory Group, Vietnam, was fully aware of this state of things. It sought to improve the authority of the Joint General Staff by recommending a different command structure which would have brought the Ministry of Defense and General Staff closer together both physically and in command relationship. This recommendation was rejected by President Diem, however. True to the nature of an autocratic ruler, he did not want any one individual other than

---

[7] The Secretary of State for Defense acted on President Diem's behalf and was practically the Minister of Defense, although this position was titularly held by the President himself.

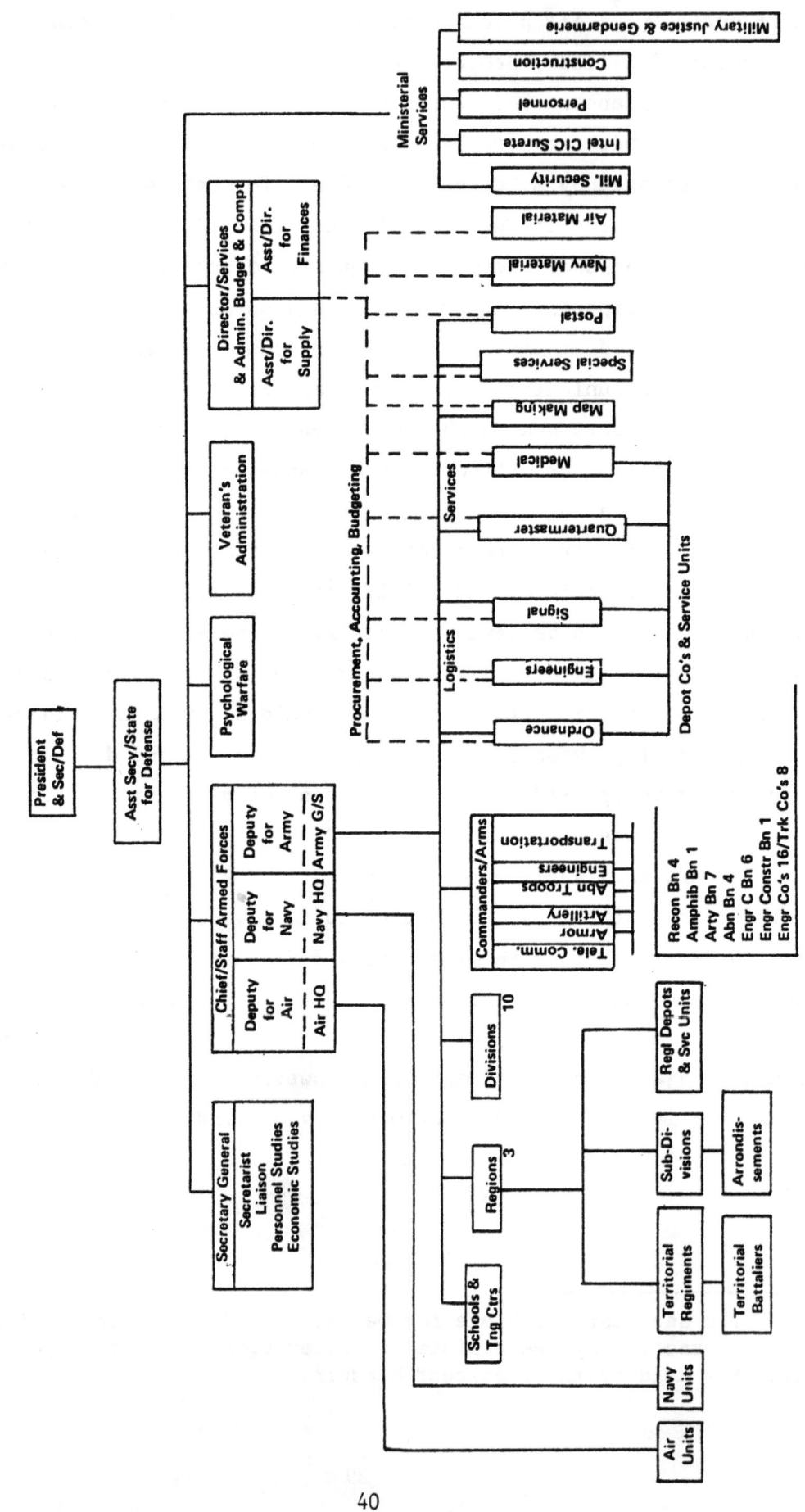

Chart 1 — Organization, Vietnamese Armed Forces, 1955

himself to wield too much authority. He preferred to maintain a system
of power division in which all subordinates should remain personally
loyal to him. Despite objections from the MAAG, President Diem persisted
in this practice.

Although it failed to bring about an improvement in the Vietnamese
command structure, MAAG's advice was well heeded in the areas of training
and equipment. The Chief, MAAG, Lt. General Samuel Williams constantly
kept President Diem personally informed of the status of Vietnamese units,
based on inspection reports. When he was confronted with the fact that
the Lieutenant Colonel commanding the 11th Light Division was negligent
in the maintenance of his divisional equipment, President Diem promptly
ordered his removal.

Operations Against the Binh Xuyen and Rebellious Religious Sects

After regaining full control of the armed forces and initiating
reorganization plans, the South Vietnamese government turned its attention to the thorny problems of suppressing armed rebellions by religious
sects such as the Hoa Hao in the Mekong Delta and removing the Binh
Xuyen gang from the police organizations. These operations provided
the opportunity for emergent field commanders to prove their tactical
resourcefulness and military leadership.

Since early 1948 when he disassociated himself from the Viet Minh
and cooperated with the French, Mr. Le Van Vien, alias Bay Vien, had
proved extremely effective in the employment of his forces, called the
Binh Xuyen, to destroy the Viet Minh's underground organizations in
the Saigon-Cholon area. The French trusted him and gave him and the
Binh Xuyen complete control over the Saigon-Cholon area, to include the
Rung Sat mangrove redoubt and the waterway connecting the sea with the
Saigon harbor. The Binh Xuyen thus enjoyed several exclusive privileges
in commerce, for example a virtual monopoly to cut timber, to provide
river transportation services, and to operate bus lines from Saigon to
Vung Tau and provinces of the Mekong Delta. They were also authorized
to operate two notorious casinos, "The Great World" in Cholon and Kim

Chung, and a big brothel in Saigon. All profits that the Binh Xuyen made in these operations were used to maintain and develop their forces.

Public opinion was greatly concerned, however, when Chief of State Bao Dai made Bay Vien a brigadier general and later appointed Lai Huu Sang, one of the latter's proteges, Director General of National Police and Security. Rumors had it that the Binh Xuyen had bribed their way into key governmental positions and that the government or Prime Minister Buu Loc had received the hefty sum of 40 million piasters in these transactions.

The Binh Xuyen forces consisted of about 2,000 troops organized into five battalions, 1,500 crack "assault police" troopers making up two battalions, and approximately 10,000 followers, all members of the so-called "Popular Front." The 1,500 crack assault police troopers of the Binh Xuyen manned 21 police stations scattered about Saigon-Cholon.

In early 1955, Prime Minister Ngo Dinh Diem decided to crack down on the Binh Xuyen's infamous operations. This was in keeping with his proclaimed policy of uniting the armed forces and eradicating all social vices. He refused to extend the licenses for gambling casinos and brothels, forcing Bay Vien to close them down. After the loss of these lucrative operations, Bay Vien reacted just like any warlord deprived of his privileges. He joined forces with the Cao Dai and Hoa Hao religious sects, which also found themselves in the same position, to form a political alliance seeking to overthrow Diem's government. The Cao Dai and Hoa Hao private armies, which had enjoyed feudal autonomy and financial support from the French, were now ordered to disband and to be incorporated into the national armed forces. This was the last thing they would want to happen. The alliance of the Binh Xuyen, Cao Dai and Hoa Hao was manifested by the creation of the "Front for the Unification of All National Forces." On 21 March, 1955, this Front passed a resolution, which sounded like an ultimatum, demanding Prime Minister Diem to form a new cabinet within five days. The resolution was signed by Pham Cong Tac head of the Cao Dai sect, Lieutenant Generals Tran Van Soai and Nguyen Thanh Phuong, and Major Generals Le Van Vien, Lam Thanh Nguyen, Le Quang Vinh and Trinh Minh The.

Prime Minister Diem remained undisturbed by this demand. He maintained his position that all political problems should wait until after the national armed forces had been unified. Frustrated by his unyielding stance, all the Cao Dai and Hoa Hao who served as Diem's cabinet members tendered their resignation. Diem's own Secretary of State for Defense, Ho Thong Minh, whom he had appointed, also resigned in protest.

However, the Binh Xuyen-Cao Dai-Hoa Hao political alliance was not strong and determined enough to overthrow Mr. Diem. In the meantime, attracted by Diem's courage and leadership, several groups of dissident Hoa Hao and Cao Dai rallied to the government. These included 3,500 men under Colonel Nguyen Van Hue and another 1,500 under Major Nguyen Day, of the Hoa Hao, and other Cao Dai armed elements under Trinh Minh The; The had rallied to Mr. Diem in late 1954 and served as a major general of the national forces. Lt. Gen. Nguyen Thanh Phuong, the spokesman of the Front itself also rallied to the government four weeks after the resolution was passed. Only the Binh Xuyen remained recalcitrant and determined to oppose Mr. Diem.

The Binh Xuyen's opposition soon turned into armed rebellion. The first provocation by the Binh Xuyen took place on midnight 30 March 1955 when a group of assault police attacked a police station and the General Staff headquarters on Tran Hung Dao boulevard with the support of machine guns and recoilless rifles installed in nearby buildings. This attack was not successful and the Binh Xuyen element was driven away two hours later by governmental forces from the Saigon-Cholon Subdivision. Both sides suffered a few casualties, and a cease-fire was declared at 2:30 am.

After the incident, the French High Command ordered its troops to occupy key areas in the city under the pretext of protecting French nationals and installations. A few areas were declared off-limits to governmental forces, to include the area under the Binh Xuyen's control. At the same time the governmental forces met with shortages in ammunition and fuel, whose supply was still provided by French forces. The Vietnamese armed forces were also ordered not to provoke the Binh Xuyen.

During the month that followed the incident, the Binh Xuyen reinforced the defenses of their areas and continued to provoke governmental forces by kidnapping individual servicemen and harassing military installations by sniper fire or grenades. The situation became more tense when Prime Minister Diem appointed Colonel Nguyen Ngoc Le as Director General of the National Police in place of Lai Huu Sang, a Binh Xuyen man. On 28 April 1955, a small group of soldiers passing by the Petrus Ky High School were fired upon by the Binh Xuyen's Assault Police inside. Irated by this provocative act, the Vietnamese paratroopers retaliated by attacking the Binh Xuyen position. The fighting lasted throughout the afternoon, and by the next morning the Binh Xuyen had to fall back to their redoubt on the other side of the Y Bridge. During that day, the Vietnamese paratroopers controlled the entire Cholon area and maneuvered into positions facing the Binh Xuyen along the Double Canal. In Saigon, governmental forces also restored complete control after clearing all Binh Xuyen-held positions.

At the height of this crisis, on 29 April 1955 Chief of State Bao Dai summoned Prime Minister Diem and Major General Le Van Ty, Chief of the General Staff, to France for consultation. By the same message, Bao Dai also appointed Major General Nguyen Van Vy as Commander-in-Chief of the Vietnamese National Armed Forces. Disregarding Bao Dai's orders, Prime Minister Diem decided that he and the Chief of the General Staff could not afford to leave the country, even temporarily, in the midst of this situation. He also ignored Bao Dai's orders to replace General Le Van Ty, an unnecessary change that only added to the present crisis.

On 30 April, a group of approximately 200 people acting on behalf of the "national revolutionary forces" met at the City Hall and passed a resolution urging action to remove Bao Dai. In the afternoon, Major General Nguyen Van Vy, Bao Dai's newly designated Chief of the General Staff, reported to the Independence Palace accompanied by Colonel Nguyen Tuyen, Commander of the Imperial Guard, to officiate his new appointment. At the palace, he was overwhelmed and chased away by General Trinh Minh The and members of the National Revolutionary Forces (later called People's Council for Revolution). Fearing for his life, General Vy fled to France the next day.

During the period from 30 April to 3 May 1955, governmental forces, composed primarily of the Airborne Brigade, recruit units of Training Center No. 1, a few battalions of the Saigon-Cholon Subdivision, and General Trinh Minh The's Regiment No. 60, attacked the Binh Xuyen stronghold and drove their forces away from Cholon. The Binh Xuyen resisted weakly; some of them surrendered, and the bulk of their forces withdrew into the mangrove area of Rung Sat. During a battle at the Tan Thuan Dong Bridge, Major General Trinh Minh The was killed. Prime Minister Diem promoted him posthumously to the rank of lieutenant general and accorded him the full honors of an official funeral.

From their redoubt in Rung Sat, the Binh Xuyen continued harassing governmental outposts located on the periphery of this area. These activities also impeded shipping movements on the Saigon River. For a short time the Binh Xuyen managed to survive because the government was concentrating its operational efforts against the Hoa Hao in the Mekong Delta. Not until 21 September 1955 did the government take military action to eliminate the Binh Xuyen when Operation Hoang Dieu was launched under the command of Colonel Duong Van Minh, then Commander of the Saigon-Cholon Subdivision.

The objectives of this operation were to destroy the Binh Xuyen's remnant forces, their bases, and supplies and to clear the Saigon River from Nha Be to Vung Tau, restoring normal commercial traffic on this waterway. *(Map 1)*

To destroy the Binh Xuyen forces, which were scattered over the mangrove jungles and swamps of the Rung Sat area, the operational command first established blocking positions surrounding the entire area of operation. Forces of the Eastern Zone subdivision were employed for this purpose. The blocking forces consisted of:

(1) The Bien Hoa task force, which was composed of 2 battalions and an armored cavalry troop, deployed as a screen on the northwestern side of the area.

(2) The Ba Ria task force, also composed of 2 battalions and an armored cavalry troop, which formed a screen on the eastern side of the area.

(3) A territorial force unit from the My Tho Subdivision which came as reinforcement and established a screen on the western side of the area.

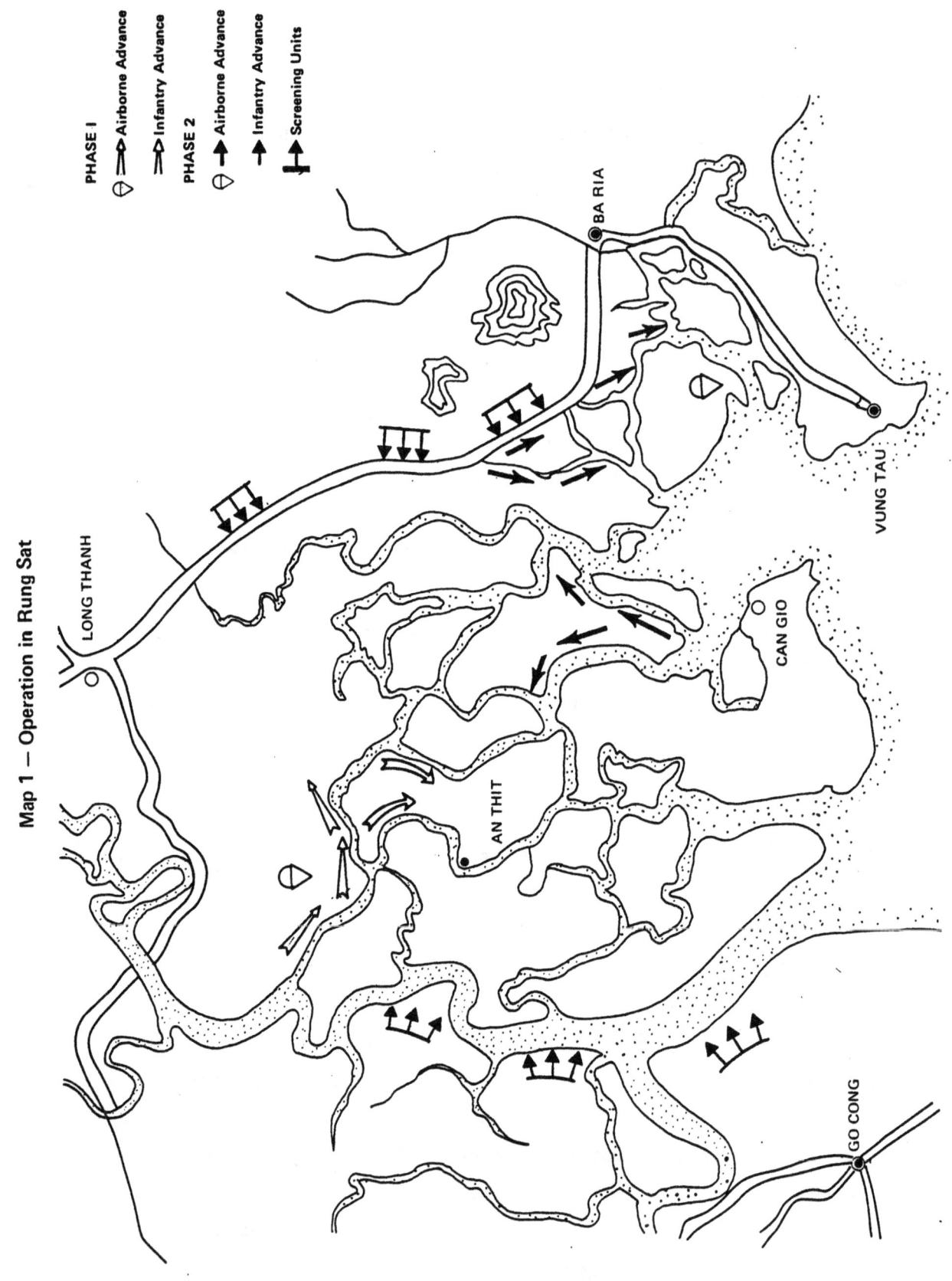

Map 1 – Operation in Rung Sat

Two Naval Assault Groups with marine troops on board conducted patrols on waterways crisscrossing the area; they also had the mission to occupy the outposts formerly manned by the Binh Xuyen along the Long Tao River.

The governmental attacking forces consisted of:

(1) Three airborne battalions, Nos. 1, 5 and 6, under the command of Major Nguyen Chanh Thi, then Deputy Commander of the Airborne Brigade.

(2) The 154th Infantry Regiment with two organic battalions, the 58th and 22d, and two attached battalions, the 33d and 809th, all under the command of Major Do Huu Do, Commander of the 154th Regiment.

(3) The 3d Artillery Battalion, reinforced with 2 territorial artillery sections and one battery from the 34th Artillery Battalion, under the command of Major Nguyen Xuan Thinh, Commander of the 3d Artillery Battalion.

(4) A company of M-2 boats operated by the engineers to provide supply, liaison and water storage facilities.

In addition, four observation planes were assigned to the operational command.

After the blocking forces had established their positions on the encirclement belt, the attacking forces began to move into the area in several increments transported by naval craft. The landing of governmental troops was completed during 23 and 24 September, 1955, but no contact was made. The airborne units landed on the Long Tao and Dong Tranh areas while the 154th Regiment landed in the Vam Sat River area. During this initial stage of the operation, all activities took place in the western area of Rung Sat.

After landing, the governmental troops moved inward along the waterways. Progress was extremely slow since troops had to wade along swampy banks in deep mud. All elements advanced only about 1 or 2 km in depth, then bivouaced on dry land and established positions to control the accesses from rivers and canals. The operational command's plan was to block all of the accesses inland provided by the channels in this swampy area. Every day, the governmental forces conducted patrols deep inside the area to search for the enemy and posted control parties at channel access points to prevent boats from entering the area and to search those that came out of it. Boat traffic in this area was primarily an activity of the local population whose livelihood was to cut wood to make charcoal. The operational command was concerned that the Binh Xuyen might take advantage of this boat traffic to resupply and communicate with Saigon.

The only skirmish of the entire operation took place on 27 September 1955 at Rach La when the Binh Xuyen sank one of the government's naval boats with 57-mm recoilless rifle fire. A marine unit was immediately dispatched to the area from where the fire came, and an entire platoon of the Binh Xuyen was destroyed.

The tactic that the operational command used throughout the operation was to encircle the Binh Xuyen, sever their supply lines, and conduct attacks by fire against suspected troop locations, usually at river mouths, channel junctions and along trafficable waterways. An average of 700 artillery rounds was expended per day, mostly with fuses timed to explode overhead. Coverage by observation planes was thorough and permanent during daytime. It was valuable in guiding our artillery fire on suspect boats moving in the enemy-held area. Several Binh Xuyen boats were thus sunk during the operation.

The governmental forces enjoyed another tactical advantage by using the high ground of An Thit for artillery positions. An Thit was in fact the only high ground located in the very midst of the area. From there, government artillery pieces could cover the entire area in every direction. This fire coverage therefore provided the Binh Xuyen no safe havens.

Just one week after the governmental forces encircled and bombarded the area, the Binh Xuyen troops began to surrender. The first unit to do so was an entire outpost garrison located 2 km inside the Vam Sat river mouth. The Binh Xuyen troops who rallied to the government told several stories of privations and disenchantment. In fact, from the time they withdrew into the Rung Sat area, few of them had any heart for continuing the fight, being separated from their families and suffering from malnutrition. The Binh Xuyen unit commanders suspected one another and were all inclined to surrender, except a few die-hard criminals.

From their stories, it was also known that as soon as the Binh Xuyen reached Rung Sat, their leader, Bay Vien, reorganized his forces into four battalions, totalling about 1,200 men, 2 separate companies and 2 others for the protection of his headquarters. Bay Vien installed his command post on a boat. Even though the Binh Xuyen found Rung Sat a safe haven, they could not stay deep inside the mangrove jungles because of difficulties in moving about. The needs for resupply, movement and observation forced them to establish positions near the river mouths and channel accesses, concealed under foliage and bushes. Their troops lived in primitively erected pile houses nearby to provide protection against the elements and tides. As a result, they had become targets for artillery fire, which was accurately concentrated on their positions. Demoralized and under constant bombardment by governmental forces, the Binh Xuyen disintegrated rapidly.

On 7 October, airborne units and the 154th Regiment redeployed from the western section of Rung Sat after having completely pacified the area. They moved into the eastern section and continued their search there. During this stage, the paratroopers acted as blocking forces while the 154th Regiment was transported by naval craft to the Can Gio estuary and from there its units progressed northward along the Nga Bay River to conduct search activities on both sides of the river.

By the time this second phase of the operation was initiated the Binh Xuyen had disintegrated and most of their troops had rallied to the government. Only a small number was taken as prisoners. The search operations conducted in this phase resulted in the arrest of the Binh Xuyen's last remnants. While all of his troops were either detained or rallied to the government, the Binh Xuyen chieftain, Bay Vien, and a few of his collaborators, such as Lai Huu Tai and Lai Huu Sang, managed to slip out of Rung Sat and later escaped to France.

The Hoang Dieu operation thus completely destroyed the Binh Xuyen. Statistics showed that they suffered 20 killed, 221 detained and 1,199 rallied. Governmental forces seized the entire Binh Xuyen arsenal which consisted of 11 recoilless rifles, six 81-mm mortars, ten 60-mm mortars, 14 rocket launchers, four 20-mm cannons, 35 machineguns, 110 automatic rifles, 343 submachineguns, 1,046 rifles, 4 grenade launchers and 75 pistols. Other materials seized from the Binh Xuyen included a radio transmitter and 30 assorted boats and ships. On the government side, the Vietnamese National Armed Forces suffered 10 killed and 59 wounded with one naval craft sunk and four others damaged.

After this victorious campaign, Colonel Duong Van Minh was promoted to major general. Many other officers and troops of the operational units were also promoted or decorated. On 6 November 1955, the victorious force returned to Saigon and paraded amidst cheers and jubilations of the population

At this time, however, the campaign conducted in the Mekong Delta to eliminate the rebellious Hoa Hao elements still fell short of its objectives even after six months of operation. Code-named Dinh Tien Hoang, this campaign had begun on 23 May 1955 under the command of Colonel Duong Van Duc with the commitment of 12 infantry battalions and territorial forces. The governmental forces achieved some military success after disrupting the opposing units and destroying their installations and combat morale but at the same time they also alienated the local population with their harsh and indiscriminating methods. It was widely believed then that the government wanted to annihilate all religious sects without discrimination or mercy. As a result, President Diem ordered Maj. Gen. Duong Van Minh, the victor of the Binh Xuyen, to take over the conduct of operations.

As soon as General Minh established his field command post, which was called Headquarters, Combined Western and Dong Thap Combat Zones, in Long Xuyen Province, he initiated a new operational campaign, code-named Nguyen Hue, on 1 January 1956. This campaign sought to achieve the following objectives:

(1) To solve the problem of Tran Van Soai, Ba Cut and dissident elements of religious sects.

(2) To destroy Viet Minh organizations and their planted cadres in the Mekong Delta.

(3) To reestablish government control over the Dong Thap and Ca Mau areas and to develop roads, bridges, and military outposts in these areas.

Since the scope of his mission was so large and the area of responsibility encompassed so many different locations, General Minh decided to assign a different area of operation for each of his subordinate commanders, in order to deal effectively with each group of dissidents.

Thus, the western Zone, which was the area of operation of the on-going Dinh Tien Hoang Campaign, remained under Colonel Duong Van Duc. Lt. Colonel Nguyen Van La was assigned the Dong Thap Combat Zone while the Vinh Long area was placed under the command of Colonel Nguyen Van Quang.

The government committed in the Nguyen Hue campaign a sizeable force which also included naval and air force units.

Army units included four infantry divisions and territorial regiments. The 4th Field Division and the 11th Light Division were assigned to the Western Zone area of operation while the 14th and 15th Light Divisions were assigned to the Dong Thap area of operation.

Naval forces consisted of four Naval Assault Divisions, the 21st, 22d, 23d, and 24th, and two LSIL, one LSSL and three LCU. Because of its terrain, the Dong Thap area of operation was assigned three naval assault divisions, one LCU and 20 M-2 boats.

Air Force units participating in the campaign included one flight of observation planes and three bombers of the Marcel Dassault type.

In addition, the infantry units were supported by six squadrons of scoutcars and five artillery battalions (the 3d, 4th, 21st, 22d and 24th). One airborne battalion made up the campaign's reserve at Sa Dec.

Under General Minh's command, the Nguyen Hue campaign was a complete success after one and a half months of operation. By 17 February 1956, almost all objectives had been achieved and the dissidents practically eliminated. Losses inflicted on the dissidents amounted to 268 killed, 3,750 ralliers, and 2,719 assorted weapons captured. Friendly forces suffered 31 killed, 115 wounded, 7 missing in action and 11 weapons lost.

At the beginning of the campaign, General Minh believed he could rally the dissidents under Mr. Tran Van Soai without bloodshed. First, he directed governmental forces to encircle and isolate Mr. Soai's troops.

Then after showing the dissidents that they had no way of escaping, he began prodding Mr. Soai for a negotiated surrender. After several secret contacts with General Minh's representatives, finally Soai agreed to meet with Mr. Nguyen Ngoc Tho, President Diem's special envoy. He laid down some conditions for his surrender which were all met by the government. Then on 17 February 1956, Mr. Soai and his troops officially surrendered and rallied to the government.

The same tactic of pressure and negotiations was used to win over General Le Quang Vinh, alias Ba Cut, who was perhaps the most recalcitrant among the Hoa Hao dissident leaders. Ba Cut also agreed to meet with President Diem's envoy, but set several extravagant conditions for his return. He was finally caught by a Civil Guard reconnaissance squad on 13 April 1956 at Chac Ca Dao in Long Xuyen Province. Convicted by the Criminal Court and a military tribunal of rebellion and treason, Ba Cut was sentenced to death and executed on 13 July 1956 at Can Tho.

Eliminating the dissidents was perhaps not too difficult a problem for the government since the rebellious forces were no match for the governmental forces. But the same governmental forces who had defeated the Binh Xuyen, the Cao Dai and the Hoa Hao, did not have the same self-assurance when it came time to confront the Communists. The following event proved that defeat was often the result of poor leadership.

Performance of the 7th Division in the Battle of Ap Bac

While in command of the 7th Infantry Division, Major General Huynh Van Cao initiated a pattern of activity which in time became an established routine for the division. He would commemorate every important national event such as the National Day or President Diem's birthday by conducting an operation of political significance. When he left the 7th Division to command IV Corps, General Cao was replaced by Colonel Bui Dinh Dam, also a presidential appointee like himself. Both were Roman Catholic, loyal to the regime and no doubt high-ranking members of the all-powerful Can Lao Party.

Soon after becoming commander of the 7th Division, Colonel Dam thought of a military exploit which could be offered to President Diem as a present on his birthday, 3 January, 1963. It so happened that two days before that, an observation plane had spotted about 100 VC in the village of Ap Bac in Dinh Tuong Province. This surely looked like an easy win and Colonel Dam decided to launch an operation the next day, 2 January after some planning. During the previous night, he landed an element of his division on an area north of the Ap Bac Village. At the same time, a second element moved to south of the village by trucks while a third element established a screen on the highway east of the village. For this operation, Colonel Dam had committed three battalions of the 12th Regiment, two ranger companies, four Civil Guard Companies, 13 M-114 APC's and six 105-mm howitzers.

At 0600 hours, after all ARVN elements had taken up their assigned positions around the village, the operation began with half an hour of intense preparatory fire against the target by the air force and artillery. Then Colonel Dam gave the orders for an infantry assault which was conducted by two Civil Guard companies. The enemy force inside the village was estimated at about 200, well entrenched in communication trenches, foxholes and defense positions. This preparedness indicated that perhaps the enemy had advance information on the ARVN operation. Not until our troops had progressed near the village did the enemy open fire. From the very first minutes of the engagement, 40 of the government troops had been put out of action. Overwhelmed by a heavy fire from the village, the two Civil Guard Companies fell back and two others made the assault. The enemy employed the same tactic: he would wait until the troops came to close proximity of the village and only then would he open fire. After the failure of the two initial infantry assaults, the 7th Division commander decided to land new troops in the village by helicopters. Three helicopters with ARVN troops aboard were immediately downed by enemy 37-mm antiaircraft fire; others were forced to a safer altitude. In a second landing attempt, two more helicopters were downed and the landing was aborted. During the following hour, the 7th Division launched simultaneous attacks from the south, the north and the east, but they all ended in failure. The next phase of attacks by ARVN forces involved four companies which had not been previously committed; still they made no significant headway.

By this time, the IV Corps commander had flown in to observe the battle and perhaps to give Colonel Dam a helping hand. A new phase of attack began with 20 minutes of artillery preparatory fire on enemy positions; well over 200 rounds were expended. This time, the 7th Division commander employed a total of eight companies for the assault against the village. The ARVN troops attacked desperately but in vain. Finally, it was decided to spearhead the attack by armored personnel carriers with infantry troops aboard and following in their wake. The enemy still persisted in employing the same tactic. When the armored personnel carriers came to within range, four of them received direct hits and caught fire; four others were damaged. The final attack thus came to a complete stop.

In the face of continued failure, IV Corps requested the JGS for reinforcements. In the afternoon, it was decided to airdrop a battalion of paratroopers over the target area. The battalion was the only reserve force left at that time, the three other airborne battalions and the brigade commander were being committed to an operation in War Zone C in Tay Ninh Province. From the way the enemy reacted to the airdrop operation, there was a possibility that our communications had been intercepted and the enemy had known our airdrop plan and even the drop zone as well in advance. As a result, as soon as our paratroopers left the airplanes and were dangling in the air, they were immediately fired upon by the enemy from the ground. Despite heavy casualties, the airborne battalion succeeded in assembling its troops upon touching ground and made an effort to carry out its mission. But it was dark and the paratroopers' attack was not as successful as planned. Taking advantage of darkness, the enemy force slipped out of the village during the night. The next morning when the paratroopers went on the attack, they found no enemy resistance at all. Total ARVN casualties during this battle, both killed and wounded amounted to approximately 400. It was later known that the enemy force inside Ap Bac village was the 512th Mobile Battalion of My Tho Province, whose estimated strength was about 300. It also appeared that the enemy had known about the 7th Division's operational plan against Ap Bac and had brought in reinforcements.

Military Province Chiefs

During President Diem's tenure of office, his administration was characterized by the appointment of several senior ARVN officers as province chiefs. This practice was continued by successive governments after him and in time all province chiefs were military officers.

The appointment of senior ARVN officers as province chiefs under President Diem was dictated by the shortage of able administrators and the insecure situation which prevailed in remote areas, especially those just recovered from Viet Minh control. By 1963, only 5 province chiefs were civilians; the remaining ones were all military.

Provinces were placed under the control of the Ministry of the Interior. A province chief was assisted by two deputies: a deputy for administration, and a deputy for security, always a military officer. In large provinces where the enemy presence was strong, the province chief was assigned a special assistant who was responsible for the two or three districts considered the most insecure.

If all province chiefs abided by the normal administrative system and reported solely to the Minister of the Interior, there would perhaps have been no problems. But presidential decree No. 57A issued in 1957 made it all too clear that the province chief was the President's representative in his province. As a result, several province chiefs considered themselves and actually acted as sovereigns in their own kingdoms, bypassing ministerial channels, and were not very respectful of higher ranking military authorities. A worst case in point was the province chief of Long An, then Colonel Mai Ngoc Duoc, who acted as if he were the President himself. His attitude resulted in serious clashes with the Minister of Interior and even with the III Corps commander.

Small-Unit Leadership

One example of effective small-unit leadership was provided by Captain Nguyen Van Tu, who commanded the 713th Infantry Battalion. This battalion was one of the two ordered by the Western Zone Command to relieve the pressure exerted by rebel units on our outposts in the Nam Thai Son area during the second phase of operation Dinh Tien Hoang (September-December, 1955). Captain Tu and most of his men were native of the same Lang Son Province in North Vietnam. During all the battles that this battalion fought against the rebels, Captain Tu always personally led his troops, arranged their formation in lines abreast and took the lead in making assaults to the sounds of the bugle. Because of his courage and this daring method of combat, his battalion soon got rid of cowardly soldiers, who usually deserted, and those who remained with the battalion were all courageous combatants.

Against the rebels who encircled our outposts Captain Tu also employed his usual tactic of deploying his troops in lines abreast, disregarding roads and marching them cross-country over ricefields. As a result, within just two days, the 713th Battalion had crossed over seven canals and engaged the enemy in close combat at each contact. Overawed by this audacity, the Hoa Hao rebels broke ranks and disintegrated. In this operation alone, the 713th Battalion eliminated in excess of 100 rebels but also suffered as many as 70 casualties, both killed and wounded. Later, Captain Tu was promoted to full colonel rank and placed in command of an infantry regiment of the 5th Division. He was killed during the battle of Dau Tieng in 1966.

Another example of effective leadership was provided by Major Du Quoc Dong (later lieutenant general) who commanded the 1st Airborne Battalion and led it to a resounding victory in Kien Phong Province in 1961. This battalion was then attached to IV Corps and was operating in the area where the boundaries of Kien Phong, Kien Tuong and Dinh Tuong Provinces met. For a few days prior to the battle, the battalion made no contact with the enemy and on the eve of the battle bivouaced in a small village. On the next morning when the battalion was preparing to leave the village and continue the operation, it discovered the sudden presence of a large group of armed men moving out of a village about three km away. Through observation by binoculars, Major Dong suspected that these men were not ARVN troops, but he was not positive. He calmly gave orders for his men to prepare for combat and waited. The enemy force now came nearer and was estimated at about a battalion moving toward the friendly positions over open fields. Now, it headed toward another village about 200 m away. When the enemy force came out of that village in the open and after Major Dong was certain that it was not any ARVN unit, he gave orders for the paratroopers to attack. Although being taken by surprise on its flank, the enemy battalion rapidly moved sideways to face the airborne troops and calmly fought back. A fierce firefight ensued which soon turned into close combat on an open field. After nearly half an hour of fierce combat, the enemy battalion commander was killed and his forces almost completely annihilated. The victorious paratroopers of the 1st Battalion seized the entire armament of the enemy battalion and thus scored the first major victory in the annals of the ARVN Airborne Brigade.

In the two foregoing examples, despite the difference in combat tactics, both the commanders of the 713th Infantry and the 1st Airborne Battalions proved to be excellent combat leaders. They both made timely decisions, remained cool when making contact with the enemy and gave their troops a model of personal courage and dedication. But these virtues alone could not bring about success in combat. They also took good care of their units, looked after the well-being of their troops and trained them well.

Observations

These examples I have selected reflect certain aspects of military leadership during President Diem's administration, especially leadership at division and higher levels. During that period, military leadership was molded by the influence of several factors. First, the RVNAF, being an offspring of the French Expeditionary Corps in Indochina, were still very much influenced by French methods of operation and the French approach to command and leadership despite the fact that they had been reorganized and trained in the American way. Second, for more than a year after they had become fully autonomous, the RVNAF functioned practically as an instrument of the regime which used them for political purposes. The use of ARVN forces to eliminate the dissident religious sects was an example, but this challenge did not provide a full measure of military leadership since the armed rebels did not enjoy popular support and militarily they were no match for the better-equipped and superior governmental forces. The true test of military leadership was evidenced only by a few significant combat engagements, and although communist insurgency was still in the developing stage, there were already indications that the command and control system did not lend itself to effective military leadership.

In the first place, the Joint General Staff, which was supposed to function as a command body, did not enjoy true authority in the military hierarchy. It was just an intermediary between the President and field units. Some of the vital functions that were needed for its effective operation and control such as personnel administration, political warfare and military security were all performed by the Ministry of Defense.

By far the most important function to exercise control over the armed forces was the promotion of officers and their assignment to key positions. But this was an authority enjoyed by the Directorate of Personnel of the Ministry of Defense and all final decisions on promotion or assignment were made by the President himself. Initially, the promotion of general officers was invariably dictated by political motives. President Diem, for example, freely handed out general ranks to several military chieftains of the Hoa Hao and Cao Dai. The assignment of officers to key command positions was also a process of clanish political considerations aimed primarily at strengthening the regime. Usually, such appointments were based on three criteria: first, the candidate had to be a native of Central Vietnam who had proved his loyalty to the regime: second, he had to be a Roman Catholic and finally, a member of the Can Lao Party.[8] There were of course exceptions to this rule but at least those selected for key positions had to meet one of the three criteria. The same rule applied to promotion which in addition to these criteria, also required that the candidate had some military achievement to show for his records.

This method of assignment and promotion naturally produced an army of sycophants whose primary preoccupation was to please the President and earn his trust and esteem. Some unit commanders even doctored combat reports, exaggerating enemy losses while minimizing their own, just to impress the President. But unless they were extremely skillful and adept, it was not always easy to do this because the President could always check their reports through MAAG or through his own reporting channels, which could be the Can Lao party or the military security system.

For the elimination of the rebellious sects, the government had committed corps-size forces, but its success, as has been said, derived partially from the fact that the rebellious forces were both demoralized and ill-equipped. In fact, these operations could be considered as simple field exercises with the difference that there was a real enemy and real ammunition was fired. However, credit must be given to those operational commanders who had proved their skills and initiatives during combat. Colonel Minh's initiative to encircle the Binh Xuyen and employ artillery to harass their morale, for example, had led to their early surrender. His initiative was tactically sound because the swampy terrain of Rung Sat did not lend itself to a thorough search by infantry forces.

---

[8]Vietnamese officers jokingly called this the "Three-D system": Dao (religion), Du (obscene word used by natives of Central Vietnam) and Dang (party).

A post-mortem analysis of the Dinh Tien Hoang campaign also revealed the skills of field commanders, who by using politics and diplomacy, had won over the rebel leader, Mr. Soai, at minimal costs to the government. At the brigade level, Colonel Do Cao Tri, the Airborne Brigade Commander, provided another fine example of courage and initiative when he took upon himself the responsibility for attacking and clearing the Binh Xuyen from the Saigon-Cholon area although the government was still reluctant to give him the orders.

The assignment of major unit commanders based on the three criteria mentioned above produced another adverse effect on the performance of the armed forces. Those who did not qualify for these positions became disenchanted; they were convinced that they could do better than those who had been selected. And among those who had been selected, a few certainly did not measure up to their tasks. The colonel selected for command of the 7th Division, for example, was perhaps an excellent staff officer, but as a tactical commander, he had proved inadequate in combat skills and experience. When placed in command of a division, he did not know how to use his forces effectively. His most serious mistake in the battle of Ap Bac was the failure to overwhelm the enemy from the very beginning with a superior infantry-armor force. His piecemeal, hesitant commitment of inadequate forces in successive assault attempts gave the enemy ample time for reorganizing and recovering. His second mistake was to select both the landing zone and the dropping zone in too close proximity of enemy positions. Also, he had directed the main attack against a point where the enemy's defenses appeared to be the strongest. In addition to these tactical blunders, the commander was perhaps not aware of the fact that the shortage of combat-experienced non-commissioned officers in his units also contributed very significantly to his ineffective infantry assaults and the overall performance of his division.

The same problem of presidential interference which inhibited the authority of the JGS also seriously affected the administrative control system and greatly reduced the authority of the Ministry of the Interior. Although they were subordinated to this ministry, most province chiefs, who were all presidential nominees, reported directly to the President from whom they also received orders. And although the great majority of province chiefs were military officers, they seemed oblivious to that fact and behaved as if they were civilians and career civil servants. Because of this misconception, some of them always donned civilian clothes, grew their hair long and were disrespectful of higher ranking officers. Fortunately, those mandarin-minded military province chiefs were only a few exceptions in the total. Many province chiefs in fact took their roles seriously and achieved significant improvements in their areas of responsibility.

But while command and leadership at the top and higher levels of the military hierarchy were to some extent under the influence of political dictates, the lower levels were not affected by it. In several small units, the principles of military leadership were respected and produced magnificent results.

As a conclusion to this chapter, I think that the principles of leadership and the virtues required of a good leader outlined in Chapter I provide a sound basis for effective command. But no leader, regardless of how close to perfect he is, can ever possess all of these desirable qualities to the same degree and always abide by all of the principles set forth. As the examples of leadership narrated in this chapter have demonstrated, I believe that every commander who wants to succeed should endeavor as much as he can to faithfully observe these principles and constantly develop the traits of a good leader.

CHAPTER III

Leadership During the Period of the Directorate

Background

Following the successful coup of November 1963 in which both President Diem and his brother Nhu found tragic death, the military junta set about reestablishing order and government with strong popular support and high hopes. Promising elections and a return to civilian rule within twelve months, the junta disbanded the National Assembly and replaced it by a Military Revolutionary Council (MRC) composed mostly of junta members and chaired by General Duong Van Minh, who also became chief of state. A new cabinet was formed, headed by Prime Minister Nguyen Ngoc Tho, Diem's vice-president, and key ministries such as Defense, Interior and Information were taken over by generals. To erase the image of the old regime, the new government disbanded the secret police, the National Revolutionary Movement, the Can Lao Party and the Women's Solidarity Movement. A Council of Notables, composed of respected academic and professional personalities, was created to draft a new constitution, but it disintegrated into futile debates. Efforts to strengthen and consolidate political organizations also ended in failure while generals maneuvered for greater power.

In the immediate aftermath of the military coup and under the new military government, the Republic of Vietnam Armed Forces underwent a radical change and were never the same again. There was a sudden awareness of political power among the officer corps, especially the generals, and anyone ambitious enough could always expect high returns in terms of money and position. Those who had taken part in the coup, directly or indirectly, were awarded with double, even triple promotions. Several officers were suddenly promoted simply by being relatives of or connected with junta members. During a nostalgic visit to his former division a high ranking junta member brought along rank insignia by the bags and distributed them freely as if they were souvenirs. This promotion spree created quite a crisis in rank value and seriously undermined military discipline and leadership. In the eyes of the uninvolved officers, this was perhaps the most irresponsible act on the part of the victorious generals, a vindication that betrayed their own ambitions and unruliness. By comparison, Diem's much criticized promotion criteria looked rather benign since the recipients were but a selected few. Gradually, the military splintered into small "centers of power", each evolving around an original junta member, and picking up new loyalties as it grew and expanded.

Before General Minh could implement a reform program, he was pushed aside on January 30, 1964, by General Nguyen Khanh. The pretext was a rumored neutralist coup by other members of the junta following an unpopular French proposal for neutralization of Vietnam. After exiling the suspected generals to Dalat, Khanh persuaded Minh to remain chief of state, while Khanh became premier and chairman of the MRC.

Proclaiming an anti-Communist, anti-neutralist and anti-French policy, Khanh advanced a program of urban and rural development. He promised a civilian government with a constitution but dismissed the Council of Notables previously assigned this task. All able-bodied citizens were ordered mobilized for military service or "New Life" Hamlets development.[1]

Meanwhile, most of South Vietnam's Buddhists sects and organizations joined the United Buddhist Church (UBC). To appease the Buddhists, Khanh, himself a Buddhist, recognized the UBC and donated land for a national pagoda. Khanh also cancelled the Catholics' favored legal status and authorized a Buddhist chaplain corps for the armed forces. Despite these gestures, Buddhists soon charged Khanh with repression.

---

[1] New Life or Tan Sinh was the new name used for the former Strategic Hamlets. The basic concept and organization of the system remained unchanged.

Taking advantage of these disruptive forces, the Viet Cong stepped up their activities. Infiltration from North Vietnam of about 2,000 per month was matched by local recruitment. Increasing quantities of Communist-bloc weapons arrived by land and sea. In response, U.S. advisory and combat support personnel increased to over 22,000 by the end of 1964. Following the attack by North Vietnam's PT boats on two U.S. destroyers in the Gulf of Tonkin in August, U.S. aircraft bombed North Vietnamese naval bases. President Johnson took this occasion to assure the world that the United States would stay in South East Asia as long as the struggle required and would meet aggression with firmness and unprovoked attack with measured retaliation.

General Khanh, apparently considering the moment opportune for establishing a dictatorship, declared a national emergency and assumed total authority. Next came the constitution, the infamous "Vung Tau Charter," which gave nearly absolute powers to the president. To this position, the MRC elected Khanh, displacing Minh. Outraged students demonstrated, joined and encouraged by Buddhist monks who charged repression by former Can Lao and Diemists.

Faced with continuing strife and Buddhist intransigence, Khanh withdrew the Vung Tau Charter and resigned. For an interim government, the MRC selected a triumvirate—Generals Minh, Khanh and Khiem. After a rest in Dalat, during which Saigon remained in chaos and Buddhists in Hue and Da Nang organized "revolutionary committees," Khanh returned to bring temporary order. He promised a civilian government and a national congress, but when he organized an interim cabinet with heavy civilian representation, the generals eliminated from power seized Saigon on September 13, 1964. Khanh was in Dalat, but some younger officers, including Air Commodore Nguyen Cao Ky, opposed the dissidents. Ky's support proved decisive, for the armed planes circling over the coup headquarters brought capitulation without bloodshed.

While the young officers exerted a growing political influence, a High National Council (HNC) appointed by Minh completed provisional organization of a civilian government. The transfer took place October 26, with the HNC's chairman, Phan Khac Suu, replacing General Minh as chief of state. Former Saigon mayor Tran Van Huong became prime minister with a civilian cabinet of "technicians". Khanh remained commander-in-chief and head of a new Armed Forces Council, while Minh and Khiem were assigned abroad as ambassadors.

A combination of factors doomed civilian government. Catholic and Buddhist groups, their differences intensified and political ambitions whetted by the summer's riots, demonstrated against Huong, charging they had not been adequately consulted on political matters. They organized student demonstrations in Da Nang, Hue and Saigon, sacked the USIS library and cultural center in Hue and demonstrated in front of the U.S. Embassy in Saigon. Promising to restore order, Khanh induced the Armed Forces Council to dismiss the Huong government in late January.

In mid-February, a joint military-civilian Legislative Council was set up and a new cabinet formed under Dr. Phan Huy Quat, a former foreign minister. Quat's largely civilian cabinet attempted a balanced representation of minority religious groups with a Buddhist majority. Almost immediately a pro-Catholic faction attempted another coup. While it failed to take over the government, the coup did oust General Khanh, who in fifteen months had antagonized every faction. Though "honorably exiled" as an ambassador-at-large, Khanh was later charged with misuse of government funds and took refuge in France.

On May 20, a group of junior officers and civilians was charged with plotting to assassinate the premier. Their arrests increased Catholic agitation and forced a cabinet crisis into the open when Chief of State Phan Khac Suu refused to recognize Premier Quat's right to dismiss cabinet officers. Unable to reconcile their difference, both Suu and Quat turned over power to the "Young Turk" generals who accepted it and installed a war cabinet on June 11, 1965.

Ten of the young generals formed a National Leadership Committee.[2]

---

[2] Members of the National Leadership Committee or Directorate included:
    Chairman: Lt. General Nguyen Van Thieu
    Deputy: Air Marshal Nguyen Cao Ky
    Secretary General: Lt. General Pham Xuan Chieu
    Members: Lt. General Nguyen Huu Co, General Cao Van Vien
                  The four corps commanders

General Nguyen Van Thieu became chief of state while Air Vice Marshal Nguyen Cao Ky became prime minister. Ky entered enthusiastically into his duties. He declared war on North Vietnam to put the country on a war footing and broke relations with France. He doubled the soldier's pay, halved that of high officials, and offered a program of austerity and reform. He also attacked war profiteering and graft.

When Ky became premier, the Communists appeared to have raised the insurgency to phase three, the general offensive. Government control of the delta had declined until the major cities were virtually besieged. North Vietnam's growing infiltration of military and political personnel and supplies combined with the political chaos in the South had brought staggering Viet Cong victories during the first half of 1965.

To help counter this escalation, the United States introduced combat forces into South Vietnam during the spring of 1965. By early 1967, U.S. strength in Vietnam had risen to nearly 400,000 men, not including the Seventh Fleet operating offshore. In addition, 44,000 Koreans, 4,000 Australians, and small New Zealand, Philippines, and Thai contingents had joined the allied forces. The South Vietnamese Army (ARVN) had grown to 343,000 regular and 300,000 paramilitary troops. The burden of fighting communist main forces was to be undertaken by the allied troops, while the Vietnamese Army would support pacification in the lowlands by fighting the guerrillas and working with rural development activities. On the government side, the Ministry of Rural Development trained approximately 30,000 rural development (RD) personnel to bring social, economic, and political reforms to the villages. Armed platoons of about 60 persons, divided into specialized teams, organized village defenses, stimulated self-help projects to build housing and improve agriculture, surveyed villagers' needs and desires, and ferreted out the Viet Cong infrastructure.

At the Honolulu conference in February 1966, Generals Ky and Thieu and other top Vietnamese leaders met with their American counterparts, including President Johnson and four cabinet secretaries. The conference placed U.S. support behind the Ky government, but emphasized not merely military victory but also reconstruction and South Vietnam's social and political reform. The Honolulu Declaration committed the Ky government to encourage national unity and broaden popular participation in nation-building by a democratic constitution and an elective government.

After returning from Honolulu, Ky reshuffled his cabinet to emphasize "social revolution" and began plans for constituent assembly elections. But the Honolulu pledges opened the flood gates of political agitation as various groups sought to seize the political initiative. A political-religious confrontation was touched off in March 1966 by the dismissal of General Nguyen Chanh Thi, who treated the First Corps Area as a fief and ignored Premier Ky's orders. Militant students and Buddhist leaders in Hue and Da Nang led by Thich Tri Quang organized massive protest demonstrations supporting Thi and demanding the removal of Chief of State Thieu.

Proceeding with his program despite a militant Buddhist boycott, Premier Ky in April convened a representative congress which recommended plans for elections and the time and manner for transfer to civilian rule. An election law drafting committee assembled in May. The Election Law promulgated June 19 created 117 electoral districts with nine reserved for Montagnards. The new constituent assembly was elected on September 11, 1966 with the mission to draft a new constitution. Then on April 1, 1967, the government promulgated the new constitution of Vietnam. On September 3 1967, General Thieu was elected president and Air Vice Marshal Ky vice-president.

Manpower and Training

The RVNAF in the meantime had expanded from 395,000 to 643,000 to include 343,000 for the Army. During 1965, the total number of ARVN combat battalions had increased from 119 to 150. The next force structure increase for 1966 was used to replenish understrength units and to serve as a replacement pipeline. By the end of 1967, newly activated units were added to the total RVNAF force structure, to include one infantry regiment, one artillery battalion (105-mm howitzers), one marine battalion, four psywar battalions and 81 Regional Force companies (used in pacification activities).

As the RVNAF force structure increased to meet the requirements of intensified war, the shortage of manpower began to surface as a serious problem which impeded recruitment and replacement. The JGS was confronted with significant difficulties in keeping up with the development trends but with innovative measures and the helping hand extended by MACV, it was finally able to achieve remarkable results.

Limitations in manpower resources were the main obstacle. This stemmed from anachronistic military service laws which were promulgated a decade earlier and included too many loopholes, making deferment and exemption easily obtainable by youths of draft age. Then there was the problem of draft dodgers, which further drained the manpower resources. To remedy these problems, a new mobilization law, called the "Citizen's Duties Act", was promulgated on 6 April 1964. This law determined that all male citizens between the ages of 20 and 25 were required to perform military service duties for a period of two years either in the armed forces or in civil defense organizations.[3] At the same time, amnesty was given to those youths who had been convicted of insubordination and draft evasion, with the purpose of turning these fugitives into recruits. Still, at the end of 1965, a modest estimate put the number of draft dodgers at large at 200,000.

For the effective enforcement of the new mobilization law, a Mobilization Directorate was created in August under the Ministry of Defense to coordinate recruiting and draft activities. A new procedure of collective call was instituted and special police operations were conducted across the country to search for draft fugitives. As a result of these measures and new harsh punitive sentences, the total

---

[3] Mandatory military service was subsequently increased to 3 years for enlisted men and 4 years for officers and NCOs.

number of recruits increased considerably, exceeding requirements by the end of 1964. But perhaps because of the prevailing political instability, manpower shortage became a problem again during 1965. As a consequence, the draft age was gradually raised to 26, then 27 and finally 33 in 1967.

Another equally debilitating problem that gave rise to manpower shortages was desertion. In South Vietnam, desertion had taken on an unusual dimension and aspect of its own because of the protracted war which seemed to have no end in sight and to increase constantly in intensity. Adding to the hazards of the war, there were economic hardships created by skyrocketing prices which made the life of servicemen increasingly miserable. Those were the major reasons that edged the South Vietnamese soldier into desertion. There were of course other causes for desertion such as family separation, and, poor leadership by unit commanders. But it also seemed that a society which was generally indifferent to the war efforts and practically protected draft evaders and deserters could be a significant factor that encouraged desertion or at least made it less culpable.

To solve this perennial and nearly insoluble problem, the JGS had gone all out in its efforts, stressing the importance of effective leadership at all echelons. The first step it took was to establish anti-desertion committees at all levels in the military hierarchy down to the brigade. The mission of each committee was to monitor the monthly strength status of the unit, see to it that all measures were properly taken to prevent and deter desertion and determine if these measures were effective enough to recommend changes and improvement.

A preventive program called "New Horizon" was initiated during 1966 to provide guidance for small units in the implementation of various tasks designed to educate and improve the living standards of servicemen. These tasks included: improving food and food service by the creation of food committees to look after the procurement of fresh food and supervise cooking and the serving of meals; creating farming committees to plant vegetables, raise pigs and chicken as supplementary sources of food; improving the issuing of individual clothing to avoid raggedness and abuse; improving the mail delivery system; organizing variety shows and competitive games to entertain and improve the physical health of servicemen; conducting story-telling sessions in which servicemen were encouraged to tell stories about national heroes of the past, about local sceneries in order to foster patriotism and attachment to the homeland; conducting personal interviews with individual servicemen to determine the problems they had and what kind of help they needed; visiting the sick and wounded being hospitalized; conducting education sessions on the duties and responsibilities of each serviceman in the maintenance of unit discipline, on punitive measures against the crime of desertion and on Communist tricks to induce desertion. As a result of this intensive program, the monthly rate of desertion decreased markedly, from 16.2% in 1966 to 10.5% in 1967.

Another problem that resulted from the rapid expansion of the RVNAF force structure, which practically doubled within just four years, was the shortage of cadres at the small-unit level. Because it was impossible to obtain experienced cadres in a short time, the usual procedure used in the activation of new units was to provide them with a nucleus of cadres taken from existing units. This was a problem faced by the Airborne Brigade when it was authorized to activate new battalions. Since there was a requirement for newly activated airborne battalions to be combat ready in a short time, several combat experienced officers and NCOs from existing battalions were assigned to them at first. This technique provided a command framework which gradually developed into a full strength unit as newly trained recruits and officers arrived. This process provided for an even distribution of experienced and green cadres in each unit but the immediate result was that all units suffered from a temporary lowering in combat effectiveness during the initial stage. The same procedure also applied to other units of the RVNAF. And when the RVNAF doubled in strength, naturally their combat effectiveness had to decrease accordingly for a short time because of the dilution of experienced cadres.

The JGS was acutely aware of this problem and concentrated its efforts during 1966 to improving command and leadership at the small unit level. A Handbook for Small-Unit Commanders was published to provide the necessary guidance for effective leadership.[4] Among other things, this handbook placed emphasis on the qualities required of a leader, the things that he had to know about his subordinates, the things he should do to earn their respect and loyalty, what he should do when taking over command of a new unit, how to organize and conduct a combat operation, how he should exercise the authority of his command, and finally what indications he should look for to determine whether his unit was well led.

During this same period, there were also improvements in personnel administration. These improvements included a career management program for officers, making public promotion procedures for officers and NCOs, proper use of efficiency reports with emphasis on education, on combat exploits, etc. For the first time, the promotion of officers and NCOs ceased to be a secret process during which debates were held in closed sessions. Now it became a matter of public debates, and every serviceman knew exactly why he was or was not promoted.

In addition to these innovative efforts, the JGS also endeavored to improve the living standards for the private soldiers in the field. Foremost among these tasks were the creation of the commissary system and the construction of new barracks and dependent housing. The success of these undertakings were made possible by substantial funds provided by MACV. For example, MACV had set aside a fund of 42 million dollars for the tax-exempt import of canned food such as condensed milk, cooking oil, fish and meat. These food items were sold back at a low price for servicemen to augment their nutrition. The income from this sale served as operating funds for the Commissary Department to procure locally-produced basic commodities such as sugar, rice and salt.

---

[4] See Annex A.

A valuable area of assistance provided by MACV was the evaluation of RVNAF units and unit commanders. It was a task performed by the U.S. advisory system which had by then extended down to the battalion level. MACV also recommended corrective measures to improve leadership at all levels and this involved the appointment, promotion or reassignment of capable officers and the removal of incompetent ones. These recommendations were always welcomed by the JGS and taken into serious consideration. Those units which performed poorly or could not maintain adequate combat strength were reproved and advised to take remedial actions within a certain time. If no improvements came about after this time, these units might face the penalty of having American support removed. This penalty was deemed necessary because MACV was responsible for the effective management of military assistance funds and equipment.

The selection of officer candidates which so far had been based primarily on academic achievements was for some time criticized as being a form of favoritism which impeded the promotion of the less educated but combat experienced enlisted men. As a remedy, in 1966, the JGS instituted special officer training courses for those enlisted men having the rank of corporal first class or sergeant who had at least two years of service and were rated excellent. By the end of that year, more than 2,000 qualified enlisted men had become officers who, by virtue of their combat records, added tremendously to the effective performance of small units.

More emphasis on command and leadership was also introduced into the training curricula of military schools and training centers during the same year. An extensive revision of training programs was conducted which sought to lay a solid foundation for the formation of good leaders at the small unit level. Instruction on the principles of leadership and the leader's qualities now became an important part of the training process that NCO and officer candidates had to undergo. It was realized that for the RVNAF to improve during the years ahead, leadership training should be made mandatory at that stage of character formation. As a result, in early 1967, the National Military Academy began to institute a four-year curriculum which in most aspects was similar to West Point's. More funds were allocated to the academy for the preparation and publication of textbooks, primarily those on science and mathematics. Upon graduation, the cadets not only received their officer commissions but also a bachelor's degree in science. Spurred on by these rewards, more students applied for admission, which by the end of 1967 showed a 40% increase over the previous year.

Other military schools underwent the same process of reorganization and improvement. The RVNAF training base therefore was consolidated and became better. The Command and Staff College, for example, admitted only those officers who had good service records and met all the requirements for admission. This was a far cry from the previous years when the college earned the notoriety of being a dumping ground for undesirable elements of the officer corps. New instructors were also assigned to the college; they were generally selected from among those who had graduated from the U.S. Army Command and Staff College at Fort Leavenworth. Finally, the college curriculum was revised and upgraded to reflect modern warfare trends and new concepts of military operations. To meet the need for a new, enlightened class of leaders, the GVN inaugurated the National Defense College (NDC) in August, 1967 destined to become the nation's highest educational institution. The NDC provided a one-year curriculum in defense, strategy and national security affairs for high-ranking military officers and civil servants selected to hold key positions after graduation.

The political aspect of insurgency warfare impelled the JGS from the early 60's to search for an ideological basis to motivate officers and men in the struggle against communism. Toward that end, one of our staunchest anti-communist allies, the Republic of China, agreed to assist the RVNAF by providing advisers and instruction in political warfare theory. General Wang Sheng, a prominent Nationalist Chinese theoretician, was sent to South Vietnam to give lectures on political warfare theory to our senior officers. Then after the activation of the General Political Warfare Department under the JGS, a Political Warfare School was established at Dalat in 1966 to replace the obsolescent Psywar Training Center. The school provided a two-year college level curriculum for the training of political warfare officers and eventually became the Political Warfare College. Political warfare cadets underwent two stages of training. The first stage was military training conducted at the National Military Academy in Dalat or the Thu Duc Reserve Officer School. The second stage of training, which was conducted at the college, concentrated on specialization in political warfare theory, techniques and organization.

Thus within the space of four years, the entire training base of the RVNAF was either reorganized or expanded and modernized in order to meet the requirements of a doubling force structure, especially those of command and leadership. During this period, several events occurred which fully illustrated the status of military leadership in the RVNAF. The examples I have selected for this chapter concern the conduct of the I Corps and 1st Infantry Division commanders during the 1966 Buddhist crisis, the performance of certain province chiefs and the exploits of airborne battalion commanders.

I Corps and the 1st Infantry Division During the 1966 Buddhist Crisis

Under President Diem's regime, the minority Roman Catholic Church unquestionably enjoyed several privileges and exclusive rights smacking of favoritism. This was one of the major causes that led to the demise of the regime in late 1963. Consequently, Buddhist influence increased, and the Buddhists eventually became a major pressure group in the nation's political life by virtue of their new political awareness. But, just like the Roman Catholics of years past, they seemed insatiable in their demands for privileges and a greater say in national affairs. And successive governments of the post-Diem era also seemed eager to give in to their every demand.

General Nguyen Khanh started the buildup of Buddhist influence by allotting public land for the erection of a "National Pagoda", which became the symbol of Buddhist predominance. Then he authorized the activation of the Buddhist chaplain corps in the RVNAF. The Buddhist chaplains, who came under the United Buddhist Church, never confined themselves to religious matters. A few of them acted as spiritual and political leaders of the units to which they were assigned. During that time, the influence of the Vien Hoa Dao (Institute for the Propagation of Buddhism), the United Buddhist Church's executive branch, was all encompassing, reaching into all levels of the military and governmental hierarchy. For all practical purposes, it functioned not unlike a super cabinet with powers of appointing cabinet ministers and granting other favors and privileges. It came as no surprise that after every session of the Armed Forces Council, the Vien Hoa Dao immediately knew what decisions had been made. Several senior officers, to include a few members of the Armed Forces Council, felt no qualms about reporting all they knew—even military secrets—to their spiritual leaders, considering it the duty of a loyal Buddhist.

By the time the Honolulu summit conference was convened on 6 February 1966, the National Leadership Committee had ruled the country for eight months. The political turmoil of the past two years seemed to have run its course, and South Vietnam was apparently heading toward stability. At the Honolulu conference, the U.S. leaders expressed their desire that South Vietnam's political base be broadened so as to allow popular participation and to progress toward elective government and a democratic regime. At home, political parties and the Buddhists in particular viewed this patronizing attitude as a tacit agreement by the U.S. to support the National Leadership Committee. They believed that in the event of elective government, surely Mr. Thieu and Mr. Ky would come out winners. This, in their eyes, amounted to sanctioning continued military rule and making a mockery of elective government and democracy. The stage was thus set for what was about to unfold in Hue and Da Nang, the strongholds of militant Buddhists.

Apparently under the influence and perhaps the instigation of political and religious leaders in his corps area, Lieutenant General Nguyen Chanh Thi, I Corps Commander and Government Delegate, who was also a member of the ruling National Leadership Committee, began to manifest his insubordination and unfriendliness toward the central government in Saigon. Rarely did he correctly implement orders received from Saigon, and he made it no secret. He even scribbled derogatory remarks on official papers passing through his desk to accentuate his displeasure with Saigon. Fearing a breakdown in command and control that could be disastrous to the war efforts, the National Leadership Committee decided to remove General Thi on the pretext that he should have his chronic sinusitis treated abroad. He was replaced by Major General Nguyen Van Chuan, Commander of the 1st Infantry Division.

Immediately after General Thi's removal, the Buddhists began to press for a civilian government. They held meetings and mass demonstrations in Hue, Da Nang and Hoi An, vocally demanding the immediate resignation of Generals Thieu and Ky. Gradually, the Buddhist-led opposition picked up momentum and spread to Nha Trang and Saigon. Most disturbing to the central government was the fact that in Da Nang, ARVN personnel, civil servants, and dock workers also took part in anti-government demonstrations. Port activities in Da Nang were practically suspended and military activities also came to a standstill. In Saigon, demonstrators were more violent; they broke window panes of houses, upturned and set fire to U.S. jeeps. Masses of followers congregated at Buddhist temples and the National Pagoda to listen to anti-government harangues by militant bonzes.

At Hue, the situation became one of emergency when at the end of March, students took over the radio station and closed down the university. Increasingly large numbers of RVNAF personnel and civil servants joined in anti-government activities. Local military authorities and governments, meanwhile, remained passive and took no action against the rebels. In early April, Lt. Gen. Pham Xuan Chieu, Secretary General of the National Leadership Committee, was sent to Hue to negotiate a modus-vivendi with the dissidents. He was besieged by the students, who put him in a "cyclo-pousse" and paraded him, prisoner-style, through the streets. The mayor of Da Nang, Dr. Nguyen Van Man, openly sided with the dissidents while I Corps and the 1st Infantry Division declared their anti-government stance on radio.

On 4 April 1966, Prime Minister Ky held a press conference at the JGS officers' club in which he announced that he would deploy troops to the I Corps area to squelch the demonstrations and restore order and security. The dissidents in Da Nang responded by blocking all accesses from the airport and preparing to resist. They also urged every household to display an altar in the street, hoping to deter the government from taking action. On the next morning, an airlift movement brought to Da Nang airport a governmental force composed of marines, field police, and a squadron of M-48 tanks. However, the force confined itself to the airport and was unable to act. While Major General Chuan, the I Corps Commander, was summoned to the airport to report on the situation, Colonel Dam Quang Yeu, commander of the Quang Nam Special Sector, maneuvered his troops and artillery in an apparent move to encircle and threaten the airport. In his report, General Chuan seemed to be sympathetic to the dissidents' cause; it was apparent that he was not willing to act against them. General Chuan was removed and replaced by Lt. Gen. Ton That Dinh.

To muster enough force to confront the Buddhist dissidents, Brigadier General Nguyen Ngoc Loan, then Director General of the National Police, made an attempt to rally the VNQDD to the government's side.[5] The VNQDD had strong support among the local population and its members, armed with government-issued old French weapons, were considered the staunchest anti-communist fighters. General Loan's efforts brought no improvement in the tense situation, however. As a result, Prime Minister Ky asked the JGS to intervene. Since General Loan was still officially handling the affair, I recommended that he be given time and military action should be delayed until everything else had failed.

When he took over as I Corps commander, General Dinh seemed entirely devoted to solving the crisis in his area of responsibility. But as time went by, he gradually made fewer and fewer contacts with the JGS and the National Leadership Committee. Finally, he stopped reporting his activities to Saigon altogether. It was apparent that General Dinh had also succumbed to Buddhist influence like his two predecessors. Summoned to Saigon for a high-level meeting, he refused to comply.

---

[5] Vietnam Nationalist Party, patterned after the Nationalist Chinese Kuomingtang.

The National Leadership Committee was thus faced with a dangerous and difficult situation. On the one hand, anti-government demonstrations continued to grow in fervor and extent. On the other, the corps commanders successively appointed to deal with the situation seemed to disappear from sight and one after another, openly or tacitly, took side with the dissidents and no longer responded to central control. Obviously, they had all become co-conspirators, and it was as if they had been entranced into it by some invisible force, a force so strong they could not resist. This overwhelming force was perhaps personified by the Venerable Thich Tri Quang who, as uncontested leader of the militant Buddhist faction, had been pulling the strings behind the scene for some time.

The situation became one of even greater emergency when reports indicated that the Communists were trying to win over the militant Buddhists and the dissident ARVN units to their side. There was then a real danger of losing the entire I Corps area to communist control if no action was taken in time. The JGS was well aware of this danger. If the RVNAF were to remain a cohesive military force, then no insurbordination, let alone armed rebellion, could be allowed within their ranks, no matter what religious force was behind it. A swift action was decided to subdue the insubordinate I Corps Headquarters in Da Nang as the first priority. To my view, the dissidents' strength derived chiefly from the support of I Corps and once this support was removed, the political crisis would resolve itself.

The JGS plan of action centered on a surprise move to take I Corps Headquarters under control. But for this move to succeed, it was imperative that every troop deployment be kept secret. As a routine part of its unit rotation schedule, therefore, the JGS announced the replacement of one marine battalion which had been operating in Quang Ngai Province for some time by a fresh one from Saigon. This was part of a conceived scheme to use both units to take I Corps Headquarters by surprise. Orders for the unit rotation were therefore made public but the deployment of additional troops by the same movement and plans for the occupation of I Corps Headquarters were kept secret because of possible leaks to the Vien Hoa Dao.

At 0100 on 14 May 1966, an airlift utilizing both military transports and Air Vietnam commercial flights brought one marine battalion to Da Nang airport, the first contingent of a larger force deployment which was to follow during the day. When the battalion commander had assembled all of his troops on the tarmac, he still did not know what mission he was going to carry out. Only then was he briefly ordered to proceed to I Corps Headquarters and take it with the support of M-48 tanks. He was instructed to act as if he were bringing his troops to I Corps Headquarters to reinforce it on the JGS orders and not to open fire unless there was resistance. The marine and M-48 task force then moved toward I Corps Headquarters, which it entered and occupied without any incident. When General Dinh received the report that Saigon troops were installed at his headquarters, he drove to I Corps Headquarters, but seeing that its entrance was being blocked by tanks, he went to the U.S. Marine Headquarters and remained there. The uneventful occupation of I Corps Headquarters was immediately reported to Saigon. Meanwhile, the airlift continued and, eventually, another marine and two airborne battalions were brought to Da Nang. At about noontime, Premier Ky arrived in Da Nang accompanied by a group of generals and cabinet members. By this time, the reoccupation of other military installations in the city had been in full progress. Brig. Gen. Du Quoc Dong, commander of the Airborne Division, was put in command of the occupation forces, whose orders were to end disorder and anarchy. To avoid unnecessary bloodshed, the governmental forces were instructed to use appeals and persuasion to obtain the surrender of dissident units. If they refused to capitulate, they should be encircled and isolated; and only when they opened fire were governmental troops allowed to fire back.

Soon most of Da Nang was restored to order and Maj. Gen. Huynh Van Cao was appointed the new I Corps commander. He seemed pleased with his new job until during a visit to Hue City, his helicopter was shot at by an ARVN serviceman's pistol while taking off. General Cao escaped uninjured but upon returning to Da Nang, he became a changed person. After charging General Loan with threatening and attempting to assassinate him, he sought refuge in the U.S. Marine Headquarters, relinquishing his command. General Cao's sudden change of attitude seemed odd and inexplicable. Perhaps he had feared for his life or perhaps he had been persuaded into inaction by the Venerable Thich Tri Quang. In any event, as a native of Central Vietnam himself and a Roman Catholic, he probably did not want to go down into history as the man who repressed the Buddhists of Central Vietnam.

In the meantime, Da Nang was being cleared of the last but most recalcitrant group of dissidents. The Tinh Hoi Pagoda, which was their headquarters and located north of the airport, had been effectively encircled and cut off from the outside for some time. From all indications, the dissidents were running short of food and water. One of their leaders, Dr. Man, who had been the mayor of Da Nang, attempted to slip out by night but was arrested by governmental forces. Shortly after his arrest, the dissident forces inside the pagoda capitulated and turned in over 100 weapons of all types. The crisis in Da Nang was thus resolved after a long and tense week. Maj. Gen. Hoang Xuan Lam, the 2d Infantry Division commander, became the new I Corps commander.

From the beginning of the crisis, the government had been reluctant to use military force against the dissidents in Hue, who enjoyed the support of Brig. Gen. Phan Xuan Nhuan, commander of the 1st Infantry Division. Actions had been limited to isolating the city and restricting the supply of basic commodities for it. When the dissident problem in Da Nang had been resolved, the government secretly dispatched some emissaries to Hue to get in touch with military commanders in the area in an effort to dissuade them from giving support to the militant Buddhists. To give weight to its determination to restore order in the city, the government deployed three airborne battalions to the Dong Da Training Center under the command of Colonel Ngo Quang Truong, deputy commander of the Airborne Division. This was intended only as a show of force, because the battalions were committed to combat operations around Hue.

The crisis in Hue proved to be more serious. Being the cradle of the dissident movement, the city was teeming with radical students and extremists. It was also where the rebellion's central headquarters was located. Thus, despite their failure in Da Nang, the dissidents continued their disruptive rampage in Hue. But here, their activities were more violent and took on an unquestionably anti-American appearance. The USIS library was ransacked and burned down by extremist students and workers. Hundreds of Buddhist monks and nuns staged a fasting sit-in demonstration in front of the U.S. Consulate building; the crisis mounted when one of the nuns immolated herself. The drama reverberated throughout the country and led to other self-immolations. Then the climax was reached when the U.S. Consulate building in Hue was set afire. To the military commanders in Hue, who had been backing the Buddhist demands, it was obvious that the struggle was getting out of hand and becoming hopeless. Disillusioned by this and other excesses, the mayor of Hue, Lt. Col. Pham Van Khoa, and the 1st Division commander, General Phan Xuan Nhuan, returned to the government side. The greatest danger of military confrontation was thus averted, and the dissident movement, now deprived of military support, was doomed to end in failure.

What followed in the days ahead consisted of police actions to clear the city from the remnants of the tattered struggle movement. Brigadier General Loan was placed in charge of this task; it did not take him very long to restore order and security. To further strengthen Hue, Colonel Ngo Quang Truong, now promoted to brigadier general was appointed commander of the 1st Infantry Division.

The generals and officers who had been involved in the Buddhist rebellions were subsequently indicted and tried by the Armed Forces Council. Lt. Gen. Nguyen Chanh Thi was exiled abroad under the pretext or medical treatment while Generals Chuan, Dinh, Cao and Nhuan, were discharged from service. Eventually, Generals Chuan, Dinh and Cao turned to politics, and all became senators. The Venerable Thich Tri Quang, in the meantime, went on a protracted hunger strike after his failure. He was brought to Saigon for medical treatment at a private clinic, where he remained for a long time.

The Buddhist crisis in the I Corps area having been resolved, the National Leadership Committee set about to widen its political base and prepare the groundwork for elective government and a democratic regime, the very things the Buddhists had been demanding.

Military Province Chiefs

After the successful military coup of November 1963, most of President Diem's appointed province chiefs were either replaced or detained for criminal investigation. But the practice of appointing military officers as province chiefs continued under the successive governments after Mr. Diem. Some of the old regime's province chiefs were eventually reinstated, but they no longer enjoyed the status of presidential representatives.

Under General Nguyen Khanh's administration, one of his trusted aides, a Lieutenant Colonel, was appointed province chief of Bien Hoa. A womanizer by avocation, the colonel was soon involved in a sex scandal and sued by several abused female civil servants in the provincial administration. As a result, he was transferred to Phuoc Long, one of the insecure provinces sandwiched between War Zones C and D. With his courage and initiative, the colonel succeeded in improving security in his province and bringing about other significant achievements. But his weakness for women soon earned him such a notoriety that he was reassigned again, this time to Hau Nghia Province. Hau Nghia was also infested by Communists like Phuoc Long and served as a buffer zone shielding Saigon from enemy attacks from across the border, which was only a short distance away. Here also, this individual proved to be an effective province chief who was credited with improving security in a particularly difficult situation. But here again, his scandalously amorous adventures tarnished his good image and eventually ended his successful career as province chief. To the judgment of his superiors, it was much better for him to function in a purely military capacity.

During the period of the National Leadership Committee, province chiefs were recommended by corps commanders and appointed by the prime minister. In general, the better province chiefs were those who had been carefully selected on the basis of meritorious performance as military officers. Those who were recommended through personal or clannish connections usually made poor province chiefs. But no matter how they had been selected, they were all loyal to the corps commander who had recommended them.

Two exceptions to the assignment of military personnel at the province level that were dictated by politics resulted in much criticism by public opinion. The first involved the appointment of a female lawyer as mayor of Dalat. From the day she took office, she proved most uncooperative with the sector commander and the military in general. This accounted for the eventual deterioration of security in Dalat itself. The second case was the appointment of a medical doctor as province chief. Perhaps the doctor's administrative talent had justified his appointment. But his becoming province chief certainly deprived the country and the armed forces of a physician who was much needed for his professional service.

Airborne Night Raid Against a Communist Base

Leadership during the period being discussed was perhaps better at the small-unit level, especially in combat units. For one thing, most regimental and battalion commanders were not affected by the corrupting influence of politics. For another they were nurtured by fine combat traditions as exemplified by the airborne exploits I have selected to use as examples.

During the early part of 1964, intelligence collected by III Corps indicated that the Communists were using the Giong Bau area, which straddled the Cambodian-South Vietnamese border and was located 10 km north of Tan Chau, in Chau Doc Province, as a semi-permanent base to provide shelter and rest for their troops. III Corps had made a few attempts to destroy the Communist force based there but on each occasion, this force would withdraw into neutral Cambodian territory where we had no authority or right to trespass.

Some time in March 1964, the Airborne Brigade, which I commanded, received orders to conduct a night raid into the Giong Bau Base with a force of two battalions. Since it was going to be an especially important operation, I was asked to be personally in charge. Based on the enemy's movement pattern, I developed a concept of operation designed to cut off his withdrawal route. In order to achieve this, I planned to move my two battalions by night into Cambodian territory to take blocking positions north of the base. Then an armored cavalry force would launch a frontal attack against the base from the southwest. *(Map 2)* If things developed as planned, the enemy force in the base would be blocked off and destroyed.

From Saigon, the two airborne battalions selected for this operation, the 1st and 8th, moved by truck to My Tho. At My Tho, they embarked on naval ships together with the armored cavalry force and artillery and proceeded upstream along the Mekong River toward Tan Chau. The entire trip took one day and one night and by 1800 of the second day, the 1st and 8th ABN Battalions had debarked in the vicinity of Thuong Phuoc. Thuong Phuoc was a border outpost manned by the Special Forces and located on the left bank of the Mekong River, about three kilometers from the border. At Thuong Phuoc, I gave final instructions to the unit commanders. The 1st ABN Battalion, taking the lead, was assigned a local guide who was provided by the outpost commander and, according to the latter, was thoroughly familiar with local terrain and extremely reliable. At 2000, the battalion moved out accompanied by the ABN Brigade tactical CP and myself. The 8th ABN Battalion followed at a short distance. The night was moonless and pitch-dark. Because of this, every man had a white piece of cloth tied to his left shoulder patch for easy recognition and to avoid straying. We moved along slowly, pressed together, and in utmost silence. As soon as we entered Cambodian territory, the lead element made sporadic contacts with the enemy, who just opened fire and broke away; this occured about five times. Around midnight, the local guide told us that we had reached the planned blocking positions. I was suspicious because at the rate of our progress and based on the amount of time elapsed and the direction given by the compass, we were still some distance away. But after a discussion with the 1st ABN Battalion commander and the local guide, who swore he never made a mistake, I decided to give orders for the two battalions to take

Map 2 — Battle of Thuong Phuoc

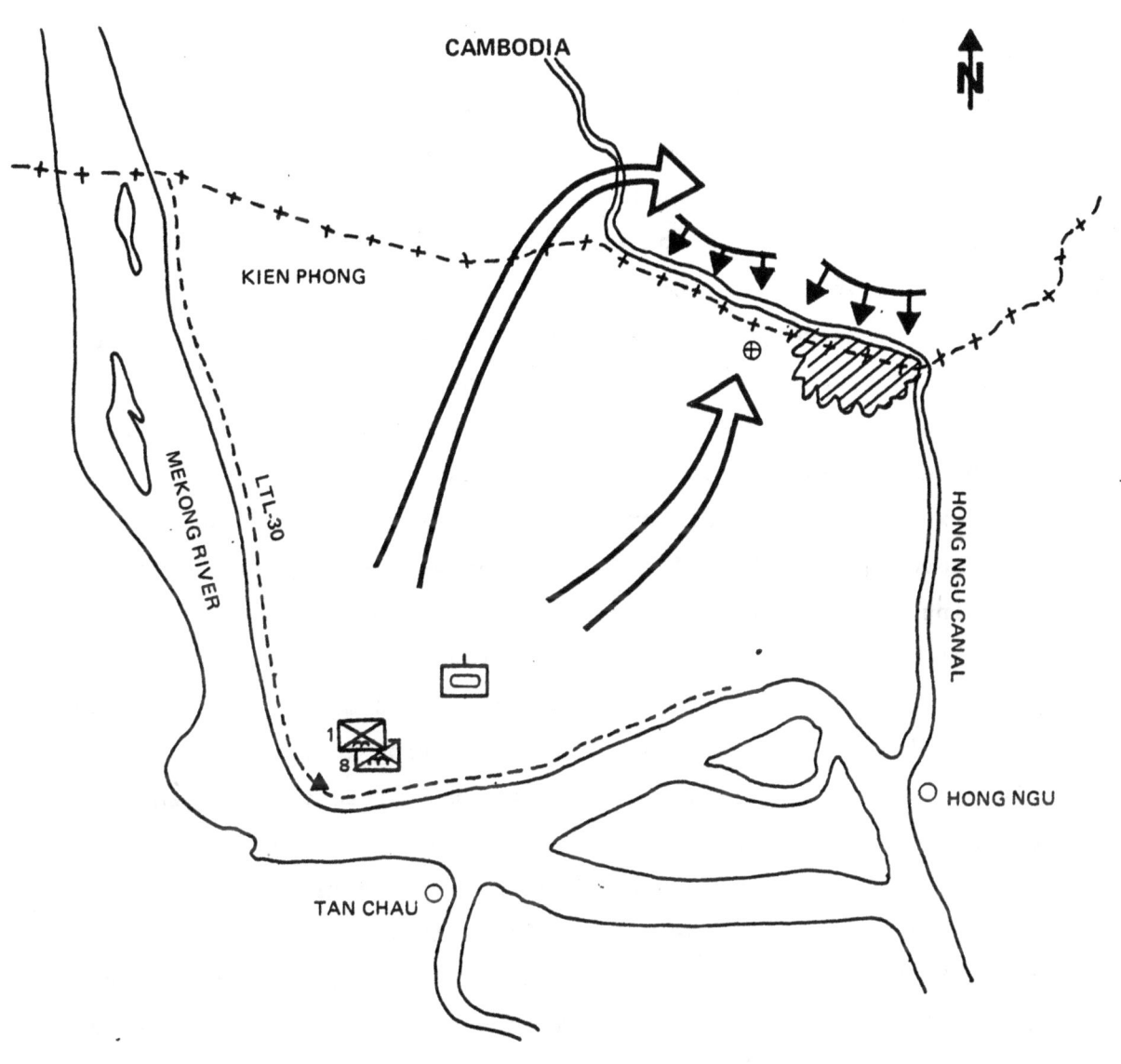

(Not to Scale)
▲ THUONG PHUOC OUTPOST
⊕ ABN AND ARMOR LINK-UP
〰 ENEMY BASE
🙶 PLANNED BLOCKING POSITIONS
-+- NATIONAL BOUNDARY

blocking positions facing south. The night was cool and our force waited in silence in an open field, ready to open fire. Radio contact was maintained with the III Corps Tactical CP at Thuong Phuoc and the armored cavalry force, which had moved out some time after us in the direction of the enemy base, according to plans.

At about 0200, this armored cavalry force made a junction with us, the paratroopers, in an open field. The uneventful link-up struck me as something very odd because in pitch-darkness, we could not make out any features of the enemy base, nor was there any enemy force coming out of it. I reported this to Maj. Gen. Lam Van Phat, the III Corps commander, who ordered that the whole task force was to remain in place and move out the next morning to continue the operation southward. After a brief search around their positions, the paratroopers settled for night bivouac, posting guards and ambushes as usual.

The next morning, the airborne force was already alert and preparing to move out by 0600. The sun was not yet rising, and the early morning air was fresh and cool. For the day's operation, I had decided that the 8th Battalion would take the lead to be followed by the 1st. A short time after the 8th Battalion had moved out and while the 1st Battalion and our brigade CP was preparing to move, the enemy suddenly opened fire. Turning to the east, the direction from which the fire came, we were able to observe blazing tracers, and enemy troops, by now discernable behind parapets along a communication trench, who were firing at the paratroopers of the 8th Battalion with all types of weapons. The paratroopers were in an open field facing the enemy at a distance of merely 80 meters; they were obviously in a disadvantageous position. By now, it had become clear to me that the previous night, instead of taking positions north of the enemy base, we had installed ourselves just west of it at a distance too close for comfort. This realization came to me as a fleeting thought. I did not have time to ponder about it because a few paratroopers had already fallen and others were wounded. The paratroopers' reaction was swift and strong, but if they remained on this open ground any longer, they would certainly suffer great losses. Without losing a minute, I swept my hand forward, ordering them to make the assault. Even my escort platoon and an element of the 1st Battalion surged forward in unison. Simultaneously, our APC's moved along, firing fiercely against the enemy's 57-mm recoilless rifles with their cal .30 and .50 machineguns. A U.S. captain adviser to the 1st Battalion was hit in the head and fell dead. As we made our advance toward the enemy trench, the fire volume became denser from both sides. At a distance of 20 m, we could clearly see for ourselves that the enemy troops were fidgeting with some 57-mm recoilless rifles. The nearest group took aim against us and fired, but the round did not go off, fortunately. One of our sergeants was immediately ordered to seize the enemy weapon. He lunged forward, firing his submachine gun as he went, but had to stop and crouch for a few seconds to replace an empty case. By the time he resumed his race, however, the enemy had fled with the recoilless rifle.

Our forces continued the assault and took the first trench, but the enemy continued to fire back at us from another trench deeper behind the first. At that time, I could see that the airborne element to my left had not caught up and was still lagging behind. I turned around and made a hand motion to urge them forward. At that precise moment, a bullet struck me in the right shoulder, but I felt nothing. A medic immediately ran forward as if from nowhere. He cut my shirt around the shoulder, applied the bandage and lowered my pants to give me an intramuscular antibiotic shot. All this had a touch of comic while the battle was raging around me.

By now other elements of the 1st Battalion had taken the entire first trench. Three times the enemy went on the counterattack, trying to dislodge us from the first trench. We held fast, but the elements to my right seemed unsure of themselves. The 1st Battalion commander immediately moved in reinforcements behind them, and they held. From where I was, it appeared that only an attack against the enemy's rear could disrupt his defenses. I turned to my S-3 and tried to have him contact the 8th Battalion for this maneuver, but he had been wounded in one eye and in the thigh of one leg. I borrowed the 1st Battalion commander's radio set and gave orders for the 8th Battalion to maneuver against the enemy's rear. But the enemy's fire was enormous and the

8th Battalion was kept pinned down in its positions. Our efforts to take the second enemy trench and destroy his forces were also met with strong resistance. The enemy not only resisted fiercely but also constantly maneuvered for counterattacks. Our 155-mm artillery battery at Tan Chau, 10 km away, was unable to fire in support because the enemy was too close.

The outcome of the battle was still undecided when Maj. Gen. Lam Van Phat, the III Corps Commander, brought in a number of light tanks as reinforcements. The enemy soon realized that he was running the risk of being encircled. As a result, he immediately broke contact and withdrew inside Cambodia. We received orders not to make any pursuit in daylight to avoid Prince Sihanouk's vocal protests. I looked at my watch and realized that the battle had lasted 2 hours and 15 minutes. By now, U.S. helicopters had arrived to pick up our wounded, and I was the last to be evacuated.

The operation continued southward after this under the command of my chief of staff. It ended with 60 enemy killed and a number of enemy weapons captured. Our force suffered 9 killed and 15 wounded, to include myself. Those paratroopers who had proved meritorious during the battle were appropriately rewarded by the III Corps commander. I was recuperating at the Cong Hoa Hospital when Prime Minister Nguyen Khanh made a surprise visit during which he pinned on me the two-star major general rank insignia. Looking back on my career, this was perhaps the greatest honor I ever received.

Observations

The years from early 1964 to late 1967 can be summarily divided into two distinct periods. The first period, which lasted until mid-1965, was truly one of the bleakest, marked by political instability and military defeats. Within the short span of one year and a half, the country underwent three successive coups and counter-coups and no government lasted even one year. The Military Revolutionary Council under General Minh was ousted after just three months in power. The next administration under General Nguyen Khanh lasted only nine months, and the civilian government that took over from him fared no better. Militarily, South Vietnam went from one defeat to another, and the situation so deteriorated that the U.S. was compelled to participate in the ground war.

During that period of time, military leadership in the RVNAF was influenced by several factors.

First, the removal of President Diem from power gave the Communists a valuable chance of winning militarily in South Vietnam. As a result, they began to increase the infiltration of men and weapons into the South to take advantage of a situation deemed favorable for their takeover.

Next, political turmoil and the frequent turnover of governments in Saigon exerted a profound impact on the morale of troops and utterly confused the population. A number of military commanders who had become addicted to power since the original coup, realized that the shortest way to promotion and important positions was through conspiracy and coups. Therefore they spent most of their time plotting intrigues, switching allegiances, and maneuvering for political prominence.

The RVNAF suffered from all this neglect and irresponsibility. Their command and control became loose and nonexistent at times because each commander cared only for his own precarious future. Military hierarchy was upset by uncontrolled promotions, which were handed out to buy allegiance, especially as far as generals and colonels were concerned. General Nguyen Khanh, for example, promoted many generals and colonels to win their support for his Vung Tau Charter. Finally, those who had served under President Diem's administration became passive and uncooperative.

The second period began when the National Leadership Committee took power; it lasted for nearly two and a half years. This was a period during which the JGS was able to play its role correctly and achieve substantial progress in personnel administration, force structure expansion and unit training. Most importantly, it took a special interest in command and leadership at the unit level. At the same time, the JGS endeavored to solve the problems occasioned by manpower shortages and desertion. This was also a period deemed entirely favorable for the improvement and consolidation of the RVNAF because with the participation of U.S. and FWMA forces, our forces were responsible primarily for the support of pacification and rural development.

The National Leadership Committee, however, had certain ways of operating which affected the military command and control system and impeded to a certain extent the many achievements that would have otherwise been more spectacular. One may say that under more favorable circumstances, the RVNAF would have been able to achieve progress more rapidly. As a team, the National Leadership Committee functioned on the principle of "collective leadership, individual responsibility." As a result, important affairs of the nation, be they political, military, or administrative, were all subjected to the process of discussion, debate and decision-making during monthly sessions. For emergencies that needed immediate attention and action, the committee would meet in special sessions. The process of decision-making, however, remained the same. During these sessions, every committee member took part in the debates, suggesting ideas or policies, and voted for decisions. If a decision or a policy pertained to the area of responsibility of any one member, that member was required to carry it out. In this way, problems were all solved on the basis of mutual understanding and general consent.

This supposedly democratic way of ruling the country, however, inhibited command and control of the armed forces. As members of the NLC, for example, the four corps commanders, although military subordinates, were the political equals of the chairman of the JGS and the Minister of Defense, who were but two more NLC members. A corps commander also served as government delegate in his own corps areas, a position which gave him ample authority in the appointment or removal of province chiefs. As a consequence, corps commanders enjoyed nearly absolute freedom of action and immense powers in their areas of responsibility, which they tended to consider their own fiefdoms. This was the major cause for warlordism and, when a corps commander joined forces with a dissident political party or religious group—as was the case with the I Corps commander in the 1966 Buddhist crisis—insurbordination and rebellion.

Viewed under the special circumstances of the aftermath of the 1963 military coup in which the Buddhists came out victors, the 1966 Buddhist crisis can be considered the inevitable result of religious supremacy and interference in affairs of state. The militant Buddhists of Hue, who had initiated the downfall of President Diem, rightfully considered themselves the guardians of a regime they had helped create. Their political influence therefore grew and expanded to the point of dominating South Vietnam's political life. It was a fact to reckon with when they decided to challenge the NLC, whose leaders, Thieu and Ky, ignored their dictates. The confrontation turned into a real crisis when the NLC leaders removed General Thi, a strongman the militant Buddhists used to advance their cause and influence. Challenging this predominant influence amounted to political suicide because it involved actions which could be interpreted as repressive measures. Since repression had led to the demise of President Diem, who would even dare, when faced with Buddhist demonstrations, to take forceful action? That explained the unwillingness of the "recalcitrant" commanders who succeeded General Thi in I Corps to carry out orders from the NLC, which they believed had no chance against the Buddhists. Besides, by bending under this dominant political force, perhaps these commanders had hoped to come out heroes and possibly become future national leaders in the event the NLC failed. It was extremism, however, that weakened the militant Buddhists' cause and led to their diminishing influence after the crisis was resolved.

The powers enjoyed by a corps commander during this period also gave rise to other forms of abuse which inevitably led to corruption if the commander sought to enrich himself. Corruption was indeed much talked about during this period, especially as far as IV Corps was concerned. It seemed as though the corrupting effect of power politics has incapacitated the RVNAF leadership at the very level where it was required to be strongest. In view of the enemy's stepped up activities, it came as no surprise where the RVNAF went from one setback to another and did not recover until politics was finally removed from their ranks.

Despite the political turmoil which affected higher levels of the RVNAF hierarchy, performance at the regimental and battalion levels continued to be good and seemed unaffected by events. The performance of airborne battalions during this period provided a striking example of effective military leadership during combat action. This example seemed to emphasize that to be effective, military leadership should stay away from politics.

As a combat arm of the ARVN, perhaps the Airborne Brigade had the most to show for its combat records and gallantry. The 1st, 3d and 5th Battalions, which were the first-activated units of the brigade, were also the ones that accomplished the most combat exploits. The 1st Battalion in particular had been cited nine times. Major Ngo Quang Truong, the 5th Battalion commander, was among our best, who excelled not only because of his courage and combat prowess but also because he was a born leader of men. During the heliborne operation against the enemy Hat Dich War Zone in Phuoc Tuy Province, for example, he was always seen with the first line elements, leading them into assaults. On the merit of his combat record, Major Truong was destined to have a brilliant military career and eventually became one of our foremost field commanders. His command and leadership ability will be a subject of discussion in the next chapter.

What then set the airborne battalions apart from other infantry battalions and explained their superior combat effectiveness? There were several reasons, but it appeared that tradition and pride were the major ones. The paratroopers had always functioned as a most closely-knit combat arm endowed with the keenest sense of duty and leadership. Their basic tenet was: "There is no mission that cannot be accomplished; no matter how difficult or how dangerous, every assigned mission must be completed." The tradition of fine leadership in airborne units was also fostered by the belief that "if your predecessors could do it, you could do it, too." As a result, every unit commander endeavored to set examples for his officers; and men, especially the newcomers, endeavored to live up to the reputation of the airborne corps as an elite combat arm.

This reputation was symbolized by the red beret that every paratrooper wore with evident pride. A U.S. adviser once recommended that the red beret should be discarded to cut down on expenditures. He was strongly advised not to tamper with that sacred symbol because its removal would seriously affect the paratroopers' combat spirit. The ARVN paratroopers fought for an ideal, just like their infantry counterparts or any counterparts in advanced countries. But first and foremost, they fought and sacrified themselves for the red beret, which symbolized their pride and tradition. I remember what I usually told the officers when they first reported for duty in the Airborne Brigade. I told them that first they had to maintain the paratroopers' tradition and when going into combat for the first time, they had to stand upright under fire to give commands to their troops, because this was the moment when the troops appraised their leaders. I also told them that if they behaved cowardly or proved unworthy as combat leaders, they had better leave the brigade, because there was no place for an airborne officer who had lost his prestige as a leader. All of these officers heeded my advice, and several of them gave their lives in their first combat experience. I had felt some remorse since then because in some way I was responsible for their early deaths. I also came to realize that there were other ways to maintain the airborne corps' tradition beside sheer physical courage, and it was better to leave it up to them and let them find their own way.

Other ingredients that contributed to the paratroopers' superior combat ability were training, esprit de corps and good care. The training process that every paratrooper had to go through was indeed an arduous one that built up audacity, endurance and self-assurance in combat. The paratroopers also enjoyed a collective life that kept them bound together in a strong esprit de corps. For one thing, airborne units received the best care and treatment available. As a unit of a the general reserves, each battalion was assigned a medical doctor who always accompanied it in combat. This was a privilege that no other infantry battalion enjoyed, except the marines. After a combat operation, each battalion returned to its rear base for a rest and refitting period, and when the time came for another operation, it was fresh and ready. At their rear base, the paratroopers enjoyed a comfortable life. Married men were allotted decent housing, and their dependents were given good care by the unit.

In general, except for a proud tradition, military leadership in airborne units did not differ from other combat organizations. The same principles and personal traits were required throughout the RVNAF to produce the caliber of leaderships required.

CHAPTER IV

Leadership During President Thieu's Era

Background

The long years between late 1967 and 1975, which spanned two terms of Mr. Thieu's presidency, witnessed several challenges to the RVN's political and military leadership. It was during this period that the enemy launched three major attempts to take South Vietnam by force: the 1968 Tet Offensive, the 1972 Easter Offensive and the 1975 Final Offensive, which climaxed in the collapse of our nation. In the intervening time between the first two offensives, South Vietnam faced perhaps the biggest challenge of all—Vietnamization—for it implied that South Vietnam's fate now lay in its own hands.

But South Vietnam proved it could survive—with United States military aid and support. Twice during 1970 and 1971, the RVNAF demonstrated their coming of age by striking across the national borders, and in 1972, they contained and finally defeated the biggest invasion North Vietnam ever unleashed against the South. Although these exploits testified to the success of Vietnamization, they also placed an unprecedented burden on South Vietnamese military leadership and forced into the open all of its strengths and weaknesses.

To understand the magnitude and implication of these challenges and the unusual requirements of leadership to meet them, I will examine the major events during this critical period of our history.

By the end of 1967, two years and a half after the U.S. entered the ground war, the situation in South Vietnam appeared to be improving and pointed toward a bright future. Politically, the nation not only recovered completely from the biggest crisis of the post-Diem era; it also seemed to prosper under a regime founded on constitutional democracy.

For the first time in four years civilian rule was restored for South Vietnam.

Militarily, the RVNAF were devoting all efforts to the task of supporting pacification and development. Approximately 70% of the South Vietnamese population now lived in security under government control. Only about 16% still lived in contested areas and 14% under communist control. As a result of combat activities conducted by over 500,000 U.S. and Free World Military Assistance troops, the Communists had been edged into a weakening posture. Their main-force units had been forced to withdraw into bases and sanctuaries along Cambodia's and Laos's borders or deep inside these neighboring countries.

The communist strategic posture had been so weakened that the Communists' chance of a military success in South Vietnam was slim and seemed to recede with each improvement achieved by our side. Because of this, Hanoi decided to change strategy. As long as U.S. troops remained in South Vietnam, there was little hope that insurgency war, which so far had largely sought to dominate the countryside, could ever end in victory. The obvious alternative, as Hanoi saw it, would be to strike at the heart of the regime, i.e. the cities, and once the cities had been subdued, the rest of the country would fall apart in a matter of time.

The Communists carefully and thoroughly prepared for that event. They infiltrated commandos and weapons into Saigon and other cities several weeks in advance, skillfully making use of concealment and penetration techniques to avoid detection. The timeframe they had chosen for the country-wide attack coincided with the short period of truce routinely observed during the Tet holidays. Surprise was the major reason for this choice. For several years, truce had come about on two major occasions, Christmas and Tet, and on these occasions, there had never been any significant activity. The enemy hoped that the RVNAF would have no reason to suspect that the 1968 Tet would be any different from the previous ones.

To the Vietnamese people, Tet was a traditional holiday to be celebrated, an annual occasion for family reunions and enjoyment. As usual, the JGS imposed an alert during this period, and all units were ordered to confine 50% of their troops in barracks. But these orders, just as usual, were never strictly enforced. In most units, several soldiers would go AWOL to join their families for the holiday, and this was condoned by most unit commanders, who believed that nothing would happen during the truce.

On 21 January 1968, NVA units began attacking and laying siege to Khe Sanh Base, which was manned by U.S. Marines. Immediately, truce orders were cancelled for the I Corps area. Then on the night of 29 January, the Communists attacked Qui Nhon City and were driven back. Our troops seized from the enemy a pre-recorded tape containing some statements about a country-wide offensive. On the basis of this piece of information, the JGS on 31 January cancelled the truce and ordered a country-wide alert. That same night, the Communist commandos who had penetrated the cities long before surfaced and launched the attack.

Saigon and other cities came under attack at about the same time. By this time, most of our combat units had less than 50% of their strength. The enemy's fire first came unnoticed amidst the noisy background of firecrackers. That the government had authorized firecrackers for that year also contributed an additional element of surprise to the enemy's initial attack. Despite this, all of our units reacted vigorously. With the exception of Hue City, in Saigon and other cities our forces succeeded in repelling the enemy within just one week.

In Saigon despite the strong reaction of our units, it soon appeared that they did not have enough troops and resources to dislodge the enemy from the city. On the eve of Tet, there was only one full-strength airborne battalion in Saigon; the other general forces had been attached to I and II Corps as reinforcements. Two companies of this airborne battalion were also attached to the Capital Military District to augment the defenses of the Saigon radio station and the Chi Hoa prison complex. Its other two companies were detailed for night guard duties at Tan Son Nhut airbase, which presently came under heavy enemy attack. The next morning, the same two companies were recalled to the JGS compound to help clear its No. 4 Gate located on the south side. Two days later, the JGS brought back to Saigon a total of 14 battalions, to include paratroopers, marines, and rangers and launched Operation Tran Hung Dao to clear Saigon-Cholon. Because of special circumstances, I took personal command of this operation during its initial and most critical stage, which lasted 15 days. By the end of that time, the enemy had been completely driven out of the city, but he still clung to some suburbs. I then assigned III Corps the mission to continue the operation and push the enemy farther away.

Elsewhere across the country, our forces gradually regained control of the situation. The enemy was expelled from most urban centers after absorbing serious losses in personnel and weapons. During this very first phase of their offensive, which lasted through the month of February, the Communists lost in excess of 45,000 troops killed. Our combined losses amounted to only 5,474, to include 3,557 for the RVNAF, 1,825 for U.S. forces and 92 for FWMA forces. The country-wide fighting also displaced 599,858 people from their homes and turned them into refugees. Damage to our cities, especially industrial plants and civilian housing, was particularly heavy.

The enemy had planned his campaign to be a general offensive-general uprising, hoping to enlist the support of the people to help him overthrow our government. The mythical uprising never materialized nor did the population ever give a helping hand to the enemy. In all embattled areas, the people were always seen fleeing enemy-held territory toward government controlled areas, which accounted for the heavy influx of refugees.

Despite its failure, the enemy's country-wide Tet-offensive resulted in unexpected developments which were to affect the course of the war in the years ahead.

For the enemy, this offensive was indisputably a major failure. His strategy had been shattered, and he had lost a considerable amount of manpower and weapons. Most critically, a major part of his infrastructure, which had taken years to build and was committed to the attacks, had been destroyed.

For South Vietnam, the Communist defeat came about as a major source for added confidence and encouragement. Aroused by Communist perfidy and the wreckage the Communists had wrought, increasing numbers of youth volunteered for military service, responded enthusiastically to draft calls, or joined local self-defense organizations. This upsurge of patriotism greatly facilitated the calling up of reserves and made partial mobilization an unprecedented success. Stimulated by this trend, the national congress passed a general mobilization bill which was signed into law on 19 June 1968. The RVNAF, meanwhile, expanded their force structure by 135,000 and began implementing a multi-year modernization and improvement program.

In the meantime, the United States had resumed bombing of Hanoi and Haiphong and increased B-52 sorties to a monthly average of 1,800. This rate of sorties was maintained until mid-July the following year. At the same time, an additional 10,000 U.S. troops were deployed to South Vietnam to counter the expected second phase of the enemy offensive.

Despite this intensification of military activities to ensure the enemy's defeat, the U.S. government at home seemed to be yielding to anti-war outcries. Apparently, the first offensive had wrought an irreparable psychological damage among the American people who, under the tantalizing effect of TV images and press reporting, were reacting unfavorably against continuation of the war. This was probably a major reason that impelled President Johnson to cease all bombing of North Vietnam above the 19th parallel beginning on 31 March 1968 and declare his non-candidacy in the forthcoming November elections.

After some overtures, during the month of April, the United States and North Vietnam exchanged public statements agreeing to establish contacts between their representatives and discuss peace. At about the same time, Secretary of Defense Clark Clifford announced a ceiling of 549,000 on U.S. troop strength in South Vietnam and declared the policy of gradually turning over major war responsibilities to the RVN.

Despite all these developments, North Vietnam imperturbably continued with second and third phases of its offensive, which were launched in May and August, 1968, respectively, with greatly decreasing intensity.

The second half of 1968 saw a flurry of U.S. efforts urging all parties of the war to sit down and discuss ways to restore peace. These efforts had reached the point that the U.S. was able to declare a total cessation of bombing against North Vietnam in late October. After raising some protest as a matter of principle, in late November the RVN finally consented to send a delegation to the Paris peace talks.

In the meantime, the RVNAF set about to exploit the gains they had obtained during the first offensive, pushing the enemy farther and farther away from populous centers. Simultaneously, the JGS strongly interceded with MACV for an increase in force structure and new weapons. An initial 820,000 force structure plan was approved together with an equipment modernization program which provided the RVNAF with new M-16 rifles, M-2 carbines, M-60 machineguns and LAW rocket launchers on a large scale. In keeping with the modernization trend, war-worn and obsolete equipment was also to be replaced by newer types. As a result, the RVNAF received replacement items such as the M-41 tank, the M-113 APC, the V-100 scout-car and the M-600 Jeep, in addition to a new series of field radio equipment. This increase in force structure was implemented without problems; the majority of the population responded favorably to the new general mobilization law. During 1968 alone, more than 80,000 youths of draft age entered military service. Concurrently, to regain control over those villages which had been disrupted by enemy activities during the year-long offensive, the GVN initiated an accelerated program of pacification beginning in November. The program ended in spectacular success after 3 months of intense effort.

In early 1969, the Paris peace talks were inaugurated with the participation of the U.S., the RVN, North Vietnam and the NLF. From the beginning, these talks were but a forum for communist propaganda, and all efforts by the U.S. and the RVN to get the Communists to negotiate seriously were met with intransigence and arrogance. Our side did not expect that it would take them three long years of frustration before an agreement was reached. On 1 February, the GVN initiated the 1969 pacification program, which was a continuation of the three-month accelerated effort and based on its success. The program soon proved to be just as successful, and the confusion among enemy ranks after their 1968 defeat contributed a great deal to this success. During the first two months of this program alone, nearly 100,000 enemy personnel rallied to our side, a record never attained before.

The RVNAF modernization and improvement program, which had begun in 1968, was also proceeding at an accelerated pace. To provide better coordination for its implementation, a joint JGS-MACV committee was established. This committee monitored and supervised the various phases of its progress, beginning with the ACTOV (Accelerated Turnover of Assets) project which transferred to the Vietnamese Navy all "brown-water" craft operated by the U.S. Navy in South Vietnam and, at the same time, responsibility for riverine operations.

At the Midway conference which took place on 8 June 1969, both the RVN and U.S. presidents agreed on a new approach to prosecute the war while striving for an early peace settlement based on the principle of "self-determination without interference." At the same time, President Nixon announced the first increment of U.S. troop "redeployment" involving a total of 25,000 men. This was the first step of a graduated withdrawal process which had been planned to be completed some time in 1973. And along with U.S. troop withdrawals, Vietnamization received a strong impetus to move ahead.

The Challenge of Vietnamization

The Vietnamization program, which sought to expand and improve the RVNAF to the point that they would be capable of taking over combat responsibilities from departing U.S. units, had in fact started as early as 1968. It consisted of various annual plans which, during the course of their implementation, had been modified several times to adjust to the changing situation and in an effort to meet the RVNAF requirements. The "Midway Package," which resulted from the June summit conference, represented a major step in that direction. Approved by the U.S. Department of Defense, this set of plans provided for a graduated increase in RVNAF force structure, 953,673 for FY-1970, and 992,837 for FY-1971. All of these plans were designed to develop the RVNAF into a modernly-equipped, structurally-balanced military forces capable of self-control, self-management and self-support. As viewed by the U.S. this force was destined to become a war deterrent in the event of peace and total U.S. withdrawal.

Toward that objective, Vietnamization progressed rapidly. Most conspicuous among its achievements were the developments of the Vietnamese Navy and Air Force, the modernization of the RVNAF logistics system, and the expansion of the territorial forces, which provided the mainstay of security and pacification. Despite a marginal increase in force structure, the Vietnamese Army kept in good pace with the withdrawal of U.S. units, taking over their areas of responsibility and some of their equipment.

In early June, 1970, a multi-year plan was initiated which focused on improving the RVNAF combat capabilities in conjunction with their expansion in force structure. This plan was to be revised every year to keep up with development trends and continued into FY-1973, by which time the total RVNAF force structure would have reached the 1.1 million mark.

By early 1972, most of this improvement plan had been completed. The biggest achievement that the plan brought about was the activation of the 3d Infantry Division, whose requirement was dictated by the withdrawal of U.S. combat units from northern MR-1. The activation of this major ARVN unit had met with initial MACV opposition, but it was subsequently validated to fall within authorized levels of MAP support.

Thus, within the space of less than 4 years, the RVNAF had expanded considerably in strength, from 820,000 in 1968 to 1,100,000 by 1972. The backbone of this combat force consisted of 11 infantry divisions —comprising 120 battalions and supported by 58 artillery battalions, 19 armored cavalry squadrons and engineer and signal units—one airborne division, one marine division, and 21 ranger battalions. The ARVN had a total strength of 429,000; the Navy, 43,000 with 1,680 ships and craft of all tonnages; and the Air Force, 51,000 with well over 1,000 planes of all types, to include about 500 helicopters. The territorial forces meanwhile, almost doubled in total strength with approximately 300,000 for the Regional Forces (1,679 companies), and 250,000 for the Popular Forces (8,356 platoons).

To keep up with the rapid increase in force structure and the requirement for leadership at all echelons, the RVNAF expanded their training base accordingly to meet growing requirements. At the start of Vietnamization this training base consisted of 26 military and service schools, which conducted a total of 326 different courses and were capable of accommodating from 24,000 to 34,000 students at any one time. In addition there were 22 training centers scattered across the country to provide training for a total ranging from 65,000 to 100,000 recruits, to include infantry, Rangers and territorial forces.

Several improvements were gradually brought into this impressive training base, especially as far as training programs were concerned. All schools and training centers placed particular emphasis on command and leadership, night operation, marksmanship, and ambush and patrol tactics. Instructors were selected from among combat-experienced officers and non-commissioned officers and rotated between training and combat duties. Despite these improvements, the training effort seemed somewhat lagging behind requirements, which not only multiplied numerically but also called for increased specialization and diversification. This trend came about as an inevitable result of modernization and sophistication, which saw training ramified into such courses as special officer, company commander, RF officer refresher, combined arms, middle management, advanced technical, and countless other technical specialties.

In 1970, a plan for the consolidation of training centers was implemented. This plan sought to increase overall training capabilities and efficiency by concentrating resources and facilities at a lesser number of centers and reducing operational costs. The 28-million dollar cost of this conversion program was covered by the military assistance program's military construction fund. When it was completed, our 23 assorted training facilities had been consolidated into 10 modern, more adequately equipped national training centers.

To improve combat effectiveness and leadership for our fast growing army, it was deemed that classroom instruction given in schools and training centers was not enough. A program of "combined operations" was therefore initiated in which ARVN units participated under the tutelage of and in cooperation with U.S. units of the same or larger size. Coordinated at the corps and field force level, this program enabled ARVN units of division and smaller sizes to upgrade their combat effectiveness and operational planning capabilities in a relatively short time. In addition, a special program of training was conducted for RF and PF units by mobile advisory and training teams. This program was highly successful despite the limited number of U.S. advisory personnel involved in it.

The rapid development of the Vietnamese Air Force and Navy generated unprecedented training requirements pertaining primarily to language and technology. A three-year program was initiated in 1970 to train as many as 3,334 pilots required by the Air Force. During 1971 alone, more than 1,000 pilot students attended schools in the U.S.. For the Navy, on-the-job training was provided under a program sponsored by the U.S. Navy, Vietnam, in connection with the transfer of ships and other brown-water craft. Under this program, entire crews of Vietnamese naval personnel underwent training at U.S. naval units, and upon qualification, they took over the transferred ships. This enabled newly created VNN units to become operational immediately after completion of training. The same type of on-the-job training applied to logistic and combat support units of the ARVN under a program sponsored by U.S. counterpart units.

As the RVNAF gradually developed and became more effective under the Vietnamization program, enemy activities declined markedly. During 1969, the enemy launched a series of "high point" activities designed to be a follow-up of the 1968 general offensive, but all ended in failure. The most significant activity of the year was the attack against the Ben Het Special Forces Camp in II Corps area in late June; it took our forces eight weeks to clear the enemy pressure on the camp.

In March 1970, a significant political development occurred in neighboring Cambodia, which saw the overthrow of Prince Sihanouk and the establishment of a pro-Western regime headed by General Lon Nol and Prince Sirik Matak. The event proved favorable to South Vietnam because for several years Prince Sihanouk had been friendly with the Communists and hostile toward the RVN despite his declared neutralist policy. His government had condoned the use of part of the Cambodian territory by North Vietnamese forces to establish bases and sanctuaries along the border. Our enemy had been using this border base system to store war supplies and materiels and as staging areas from which to harass and attack South Vietnam. Over the years, RVNAF had made limited thrusts, primarily raids of short duration, into Cambodian territory. These penetrations were shallow and largely escaped notice because in most areas of the frontier, the border was ill-defined on the ground as well as on the maps. Deep attacks across the border were made neither by the Americans nor by the RVNAF largely because U.S. policy, which naturally strongly influenced South Vietnam's behavior, included respect, so far as practicable, of Cambodia's sovereignty and proclaimed neutrality. With Sihanouk gone, however, South Vietnam was afforded a rare opportunity to move gainst these enemy bases.

As early as late March, after the new Cambodian government had closed the port of Sihanoukville (now redesignated Kompong Som) to communist ships, III and IV Corps launched a few reconnaissance operations into border areas of Hau Nghia and Kien Tuong Provinces. These local forays yielded some communist weapons and materiels. Then with the GVN approval and U.S. and Khmer concurrence, the RVNAF launched larger scale operations into Cambodia in late April and early May, 1970. During the initial stage, III and IV Corps joined forces and searched the Parrot's Beak area, where they captured substantial amounts of enemy weapons and ammunition. In the next stage, III Corps launched operations from the Tay Ninh border north and northeastward into the Fishhook and Angel's Wing areas and also helped relieve enemy pressure on Cambodian provinces east of the Mekong River. At about the same time, II Corps conducted operations into enemy bases across the border and assisted Khmer forces in evacuating two isolated outposts under enemy pressure. IV Corps, meanwhile, operated along the border and also helped break the enemy's siege on several Cambodian cities and towns.

For these operations, both III and IV Corps employed a force equivalent to six infantry divisions and three major brigades. Also, to clear the Mekong River which had been interdicted by the enemy at several places, the Vietnamese Navy, with the support of the U.S. Navy, conducted an operation from the border to Phnom Penh, the capital of Cambodia. In general, during the initial phase of the cross-border operations, the RVNAF confined their activities to a border area whose depth varied from 40 to 60 km. As dictated by requirements, the RVNAF subsequently extended their area of operation to the west of Cambodia, covering a substantial part of Cambodian territory limited by Snoul and Mimot to the northeast, Kompong Cham to the north, the Mekong River up to Phnom Penh to the west; and by Route No. 4 running through Kompong Speu and Kampot.

The results brought about by cross-border operations were encouraging. In total, II, III and IV Corps forces inflicted on the enemy 11,349 dead, 2,328 detained and seized in excess of 25,000 assorted weapons and 2,500 tons of assorted ammunition. It was estimated that this amount of weapons and ammunition could have sustained the enemy for a six-month campaign in the III and IV Corps areas of South Vietnam at the same intensity as during the previous year. These cross-border operations also made the RVNAF feel more self-assured than before and greatly enhanced the confidence of South Vietnam. The assistance provided by the RVN to its Cambodian neighbor during these operations was also a source of pride for our nation.

The situation of South Vietnam in the aftermath of the Cambodian cross-border operations seemed to promise a bright future for the nation. The disruption of border bases had driven communist main forces deeper inside Cambodia and greatly bolstered South Vietnam's security. Enemy activities for the rest of 1970 and much of the following year were confined mostly to harassments of our installations by shellings or sapper attacks. The enemy's efforts to infiltrate supplies and materiels by sea was also defeated after most of his infiltration boats had been detected and sunk.

To further consolidate the political base of the nation, in 1970 the GVN initiated the "Land-to-the-Tiller" program, which was designed to eradicate social injustice and win the support of the farming peasantry. Even though a success, the program brought about a most unexpected reaction from another segment of society: the disabled veterans. Feeling that the government had not treated them well enough while favoring other segments of society, the disabled veterans went on a rampage, squatting on unused public lands in Saigon and Cholon. The disorder took the government a long time and a lot of skillful persuasion to quell.

At the Paris peace talks, meanwhile, there was still no progress. By mid 1970, the Communists were still insistent on their demands: a coalition government, neutrality and an immediate cease-fire. President Thieu rejected them all.

In early 1971, encouraged by the results obtained from the Cambodian cross-border operations, MACV suggested that the RVNAF conduct an offensive operation into lower Laos to disrupt enemy logistic installations and storages in the Tchepone area. After the concept had been approved by President Thieu, the JGS instructed I Corps to plan and conduct this operation with the participation of the general reserve forces, the Airborne and Marine Divisions in addition to I Corps's organic forces, the 1st Infantry Division, the 1st Ranger Group and the 1st Armor Brigade. Code-named LAM SON 719, the lower-Laos operation was initiated on 8 February 1971 and sustained for 2 months.

During the second half of 1971, South Vietnam was alive with the fall presidential elections. There were at first three candidates for the presidency: President Thieu, Vice-President Ky and General Duong Van Minh. The new election law had made it impossible for other candidates to qualifiy; Vice-President Ky's candidacy was ratified only after he filed a complaint with the Supreme Court. In late August, however, both Generals Minh and Ky decided to withdraw their candidacy, leaving President Thieu as the sole candidate. This drew criticism on President Thieu whom public opinion accused of maneuvering for the elimination of his adversaires and tending toward autocratic rule. On 18 September, students and disabled veterans demonstrated in Saigon to oppose the elections, particularly the "solo performance" by President Thieu. The elections went on as scheduled, however, and President Thieu was reelected with 92% of the total ballots on 3 October 1971.

In the meantime, U.S. and FWMA forces continued to withdraw from South Vietnam and turn over military bases to the RVNAF. By the end of 1971, total U.S. strength had been reduced to 158,119, and FWMA strength, to 54,497. The RVNAF total strength, by contrast, had soared to 1,046,254.

In late 1971, the GVN initiated a comprehensive pacification program called the "Community Defense and Local Development Plan" which was to be implemented in four years beginning in 1972. This was a radical departure from pacification programs of years past, which had all been planned and implemented on an yearly basis. In launching this program, the GVN had felt that the achievements obtained during 1970 and 1971, especially as far as security and political stability were concerned, had warranted a longer look into the future and that the government should devote attention to long-range objectives instead of short-term problems.

The four-year Community Defense and Local Development program sought to achieve three basic objectives: self-defense, self-management, and self-development. As a term, pacification no longer applied because government control had extended to almost all villages and hamlets across the country. The program also adopted a new approach to development which saw more responsibilities assigned to local governments in the task of nation-building. Prospects for the future looked promising indeed since, if implemented according to plans, the program should enable South Vietnam to become a prosperous and self-reliant nation.

This ultimate goal was precisely what the Communists were endeavoring to wreck. What we had discovered during the course of protracted peace negotiations left no doubt as to our enemy's real desire to see the U.S. completely withdrawn and South Vietnam turned over to his control. But our American ally was far from giving in to a disguised surrender. It simply wanted an honorable exit, a fair settlement of the war. This deadlock apparently could not be solved by the negotiation approach.

Our enemy opted instead for a military solution he thought could help achieve his goal. All of his preparations for this event did not go unnoticed by our side. In fact, beginning in mid-1971, North Vietnam began to receive a substantial increase in military assistance from Russia and Red China. Its infiltration of men and supplies into the South also stepped up significantly, and as 1971 drew to its end, its main force divisions began to move into staging areas, particularly the NT2 and 320th Divisions north of Kontum.

Obviously, the enemy would launch an offensive in early 1972, probably during the Tet holiday period. The JGS's estimate also focused on probable target areas such as Tay Ninh in MR-3 and northern MR-1 in addition to Kontum. The only surprise came about when the enemy chose to strike across the DMZ with a multi-division force supported by armor and artillery, even though we clearly realized he had this capability. Although fully prepared for a considerable time, the enemy had waited until the end of March to launch his offensive.

The Nguyen Hue campaign, as the enemy called this offensive, was conducted in three separate and major efforts. The first effort involved a frontal attack launched across the DMZ into northern Quang Tri Province and coordinated with another attack in the direction of Hue City. A few days later, a second effort was driven from the Cambodian border against Binh Long Province in northern MR-3. The third effort, which began 14 days later, was directed against Kontum City at the same time as disruptive activities mounted in Binh Dinh Province on the coast. In the Mekong Delta, however, there was only an increase in enemy activities in areas adjoining the Cambodian border, especially in Chuong Thien Province which bordered on the U Minh Forest. But here, the enemy effort was not as strong and sustained as in other military regions.

North Vietnam thus committed a total of 14 infantry divisions in the offensive together with substantial artillery and armor forces. The initial momentum of the offensive was so overwhelming that the system of fire bases manned as defense positions by the 3d ARVN Division south of the DMZ was unable to hold more than three days. After resisting for a month, the 3d Division and other ARVN defense forces in northern MR-1 suddenly crumbled following a tactical blunder. Quang Tri Province fell into enemy hands despite the JGS efforts to reinforce I Corps with more infantry units and air support. Elsewhere, the northwestern part of Kontum Province, the northern part of Binh Long Province and northern Binh Dinh Province also came under enemy control. The cities of Kontum and An Loc were besieged and under unrelenting enemy attacks. It had taken the RVNAF three months to recover from the initial setbacks and counterattack after replacing losses and refitting their battered units within a record time. With strong U.S. air support, the RVNAF eventually regained almost all territories lost during the first month of the offensive.

In his effort to wreck the success of Vietnamization, gain a strong bargaining position at the Paris peace talks and perhaps to play on the outcome of the U.S. presidential elections in November, our enemy had committed almost the entirety of his main force divisions and an impressive array of modern weapons. Despite this, he had not only fallen short of his goal but also lost approximately 100,000 men and many of the new weapons supplied by the communist bloc in exchange for the control of a few remote district towns in South Vietnam.

Cognizant of the danger South Vietnam was facing, the U.S. reacted forcefully. For the first time in the war, it sent B-52's on bombing missions deep inside North Vietnam. The U.S. 7th Fleet was quickly reinforced with several ships to include eventually a total of seven aircraft carriers. U.S. tactical aircraft and naval gunfire attacked all vital targets in North Vietnam, to include major bridges, railway stations and power plants in the vicinity of Hanoi, Hai Phong, Vinh and other cities. Two of North Vietnam's most important bridges, the Long Bien bridge across the Red River in Hanoi and the Ham Rong (Dragon's Jaw) bridge in Thanh Hoa Province were destroyed by U.S. "smart bombs." At the same time, all major ports, to include Hai Phong, were interdicted by mines.

Inside South Vietnam, U.S. B-52's and tactical aircraft provided effective support for our troops, which resisted heroically, especially those under siege at An Loc and Kontum, and played an important role in our effort to retake the lost territories. The U.S. Air Force also contributed significantly to the deployment of ARVN troops from one military region to another and the emergency delivery of critical replacement equipment such as tanks and howitzers, enabling the RVNAF to refit their units in time for the counterattacks.

In concert with those forceful military actions, the U.S. accelerated the negotiating process in Paris in an effort to arrive at a peace settlement with North Vietnam, which was timed to be concluded prior to the U.S. presidential elections. The text of this preliminary agreement, however, contained several disadvantages for the RVN. Convinced that it would open the way to a coalition government in South Vietnam, President Thieu refused its endorsement. He was promptly accused by North Vietnam of undermining peace; our enemy insisted that the U.S. should sign the agreement on 31 October 1972, as scheduled. President Thieu's rejection thus upset the timetable that had been agreed upon by the U.S. and North Vietnam to conclude what later became known as the Paris Agreement. On his part, the U.S. negotiator, Dr. Kissinger, was convinced that "peace was at hand" when he explained the text of the agreement to the American public.

The RVN's strong reaction gave second thoughts to President Nixon. He directed that the agreement be reworded so as to remove ambiguities and at the same time, to win over his ally, decided to send more modern equipment to South Vietnam. The crash "Enhance Plus" program of equipment delivery which resulted from this decision was probably designed to reaffirm U.S. continued support for South Vietnam. It was also a move to stock up South Vietnam with war materiels before the conclusion of the final agreement, which expressly forbade it. Refusing to renegotiate at first, North Vietnam was finally brought back to the conference table under the heavy pressure of U.S. bombings. The text of the agreement was revised and finally signed by the U.S., the RVN, North Vietnam and the PRG on 27 January 1972.

The Challenge of Peace

Contrary to expectations, the Paris Agreement, which provided for a standstill cease-fire, did not silence the sound of gunfire in South Vietnam. Almost immediately after the agreement went into effect, the Communists took advantage of the cease-fire by carrying out a machiavellian scheme to "grab land and population" which they had carefully planned since October the previous year. Under this scheme, communist forces broke down into small elements and penetrated villages and hamlets under GVN control, planting NLF flags as they went and claiming these places to be under their control. At the same time, they placed roadblocks on lines of communication where they also planted flags to stake out claims. Almost as swiftly, the RVNAF reacted with vigor and determination. Within a short time, our forces succeeded in retaking all penetrated villages and hamlets and restoring normal traffic on all lines of communications after removing enemy flags and roadblocks.

As a result, enemy-initiated incidents during 1973 soared to a monthly average of 2,980, as compared to 2,072 for 1972, the year of the Easter general offensive. In addition to the land and population grab campaign during 1973, the Communists committed four serious violations by attacking Cua Viet, Sa Huynh, Hong Ngu, and Trung Nghia. Enemy actions were also directed against outlying bases such as Tong Le Chan, Le Minh, Ngoc Bay and Bach Ma. During the year, the enemy also began rehabilitation work on airstrips in areas under his control and expanded the Ho Chi Minh trail system to move supplies and materiels into South Vietnam day and night.

As to the RVNAF, during 1973 they had to contend not only with increasing enemy violations but also with limitations in the supply of fuels and ammunition. These limitations became more pronounced during the next year when U.S. military aid was drastically reduced.

The year 1974 began with the forced occupation of the Hoang Sa (Paracels) Islands offshore South Vietnam by Chinese Communists. Enemy activities during the year increased both in scope and in level, reaching an unprecedented high of 3,300 incidents per month. The enemy also kept up his logistical buildup activities along the border areas, and the ICCS continued to watch all of these violations with utter impotence. From the north-south main infiltration route along the border, the enemy was now constructing several lateral roads pushing into the coastal plains or as accesses to the outlying district towns and piedmont bases which he was trying to isolate. Several of these bases were successively overrun by the enemy, such as Dak Pek, Mang Buk, Plateau QL, and Gia Vuc, all of them lying in the way of the enemy's access roads. A new fuel pipeline was installed which reached southward to the Quang Duc area. And gradually, the targets of enemy attacks became more important to include eventually populous centers.

The RVNAF reacted most commendably against enemy incursions into these populous centers. Our large-scale operations, which sometimes involved as many as two or three divisions, succeeded in driving enemy forces away and often across the country. In the Mekong Delta, however, our forces fared less well, and the enemy was able to control several villages and hamlets in the provinces of Kien Giang, An Xuyen, and Chuong Thien. This weakness stemmed primarily from the ineffectiveness of RF and PF units, which suffered not only from understrength but also from lowered morale. An investigation was conducted by the JGS and shortly thereafter, Maj. Gen. Nguyen Vinh Nghi, IV Corps commander was removed from command.

Two years after the Paris Agreement went into effect, South Vietnam was edged into an increasingly disadvantageous position. Government control gradually shrank as populous centers came under serious enemy threat and the system of border defense no longer existed. The RVNAF exerted maximum efforts to improve this precarious situation but were greatly impeded by overextension and the effect of military aid cutbacks. For FY-74, military aid appropriations amounted to just one-third of the amount expended during the previous fiscal year. Drastic limitations in the consumption of fuels and ammunition, to cite only two of the most critical items, severely curtailed the RVNAF combat capabilities. Our units were compelled to devise ways to fight what became known as "a poor man's war." Yet they had to confront an enemy who was becoming not only numerically superior but also stronger in firepower and logistic support.

The national economy meanwhile was beset by galloping inflation and unproductivity. Basic commodities continued to be imported; rice imports alone amounted to 200,000 tons per year. Production was seriously curtailed by the vast expanse of uncultivated land: approximately 700,000 acres of ricefield and 50% of rubber plantations were either left unattended or destroyed by war. The Vietnamese currency was shrinking in value and prices soared. Its piaster, which was worth 1/35 of a U.S. dollar in 1964, now plummeted to a record low, a mere 1/685 of a dollar on the official exchange market. Along with the withdrawal of U.S. and FWMA troops, the RVN also lost a substantial source of income in foreign currency. The nation had yet to recover from the physical damage and economic ravages caused by the 1972 Easter offensive. On top of these difficulties, the world-wide oil crisis made the South Vietnamese economy even worse by virtue of its chain-reaction effect. A little hope kindled when oil was discovered in the national continental shelf, but effective production was still from 3 to 5 years away. In the face of this economic impasse, the GVN made plans to reduce the RVNAF total strength to just one million. But this soon proved impractical as enemy activities continued to increase.

Politically, the GVN also met with difficulties in its attempt to sell the Paris Agreement to the people and armed forces of South Vietnam, who had for years been conditioned to think of Communists as rebels and archenemy. Even after signing the Paris Agreement, President Thieu persisted in maintaining a hard-line anti-Communist stance when he proclaimed his "four-no's" policy. How could any one explain then the contradictory fact that, as signatories of the agreement, the Communists had become our political partners? If not, why were they allowed to install offices and circulate freely in Saigon and other cities? Thus, despite the GVN's propagandistic efforts, it was hard for the South Vietnamese people to believe that the Paris Agreement was anything else but a "sell out," a breach of faith by the national leaders. It was obvious then that since the advent of the Paris Agreement, South Vietnam's political posture had declined markedly. President Thieu's prestige suffered accordingly, and his authority deteriorated when he was publicly denounced by demonstrators who opposed and challenged him.

All these developments ushered South Vietnam into the position of an underdog, politically and militarily. The enemy wisely exploited our debility by escalating violations and increasing his military pressure. He eventually succeeded in taking the provincial city of Phuoc Long, the first one lost in South Vietnam since the cease-fire. And this flagrant violation by the Communists resulted in a complete silence of those powers who had committed themselves to guaranteeing peace for South Vietnam. To compound a deteriorating situation, the U.S. Congress reduced military aid appropriations to 700 million U.S. dollars for FY-75. With this amount of aid, the RVNAF were barely able to meet one-half of their total maintenance and operational costs. As a result, the VNAF was forced to keep the major part of its aircraft grounded and ARVN artillery units fired only within the limits of a dwindling available supply rate. The enemy meanwhile seemed to prosper and grew ever stronger. His posture had become one of unsurpassed strength, and nothing seemed to stop him in the final conquest of South Vietnam.

After the loss of Phuoc Long, several U.S. congressional delegations arrived in South Vietnam to assess the situation and to determine whether or not the requested 300-million additional aid could help stabilize it. They came away with divided opinions, and no one knew what the outcome would be. The one man who should have known the best was perhaps President Thieu himself. He probably knew that there were very slim chances of obtaining the additional appropriations, and if U.S. aid for South Vietnam were to continue at all, it would surely be reduced to a trickle.

It was perhaps his despair about the prospect of U.S. aid that impelled President Thieu to change strategy after the loss of another provincial city, Ban Me Thuot, on 11 March 1975. Summoning his advisers and key field commanders, he imparted a new strategy to save South Vietnam from ultimate collapse. Justifying his decision, he reasoned that this was the only alternative left for South Vietnam to survive, given its military, political, and economic posture. The new strategy consisted primarily of a major redeployment of forces to hold only that portion of the country deemed vital to its survival: MR-3 and MR-4 in their entirety, Ban Me Thuot and the coastal provinces of MR-2 south of Tuy Hoa, the southern part of MR-1 below Hue or the Hai Van Pass or even Chu Lao, and, of course, the valuable continental shelf adjoining all of these areas.

Ban Me Thuot, which happened to be part of the territory to be held, was to be retaken. As a result, three days after its loss, President Thieu ordered the MR-2 commander, Maj. Gen. Pham Van Phu, to redeploy his forces and reoccupy Ban Me Thuot at all costs. General Phu's ill-planned maneuver cost him over one-half of his forces and ended in dismal failure. The disruption of II Corps forces and the abandoning of the Central Highlands had a severe impact on the conduct of the war and led rapidly to the successive losses of MR-2's remaining provinces. The drama of South Vietnam's final collapse just began to unfold.

The still intact MR-1, in the meantime, found the morale of its population and troops seriously underminded by rumors of an imminent partition that would cede all of MR-1 to the enemy. The fact that the Central Highlands had been abandoned came to reinforce the credibility of these rumors and was instrumental in the rapid collapse of morale among I Corps troops and population. Fleeing in despair, refugees clogged Route QL-1, the only artery of MR-1, and caused a massive impasse at

Da Nang. The slowness and inefficiency with which the Saigon government moved to help I Corps solve this debilitating refugee problem made the situation more despondent. Finally, under mounting enemy pressure and attacks, I Corps forces were compelled to withdraw from MR-1 on 29 March 1975.[1]

After the withdrawals from MR-2 and MR-1, the RVNAF lost about 50% of their combat capabilities, but most of these losses were self-inflicted. Despite desperate efforts to replace losses and refit with whatever remained usable, the RVNAF never recovered enough to stabilize the situation. Encouraged by this windfall, the Communists massed 15 divisions in a forceful drive to take Saigon. After the last stronghold at Xuan Loc had caved in to enemy pressure, President Thieu decided to step down on 21 April 1975 amidst rumors that the enemy was willing to negotiate a political solution only with a government led by General Duong Van Minh. But President Thieu turned over his presidency to Vice President Huong as dictated by the constitution. As the military situation continued to deteriorate with every passing day, on 27 April 1975, the South Vietnamese national congress voted to turn over the presidency to General Duong Van Minh. General Minh took office on the afternoon of 28 April. Unable to negotiate a political solution with the Communists, he ordered the RVNAF to capitulate on the morning of 30 April 1975.

South Vietnam thus ceased to exist as a nation. As the events which precipitated its early demise had proven, the nation's ultimate failure was also one of leadership. Throughout the years of its existence, South Vietnam always depended on its armed forces for survival. This dependence was particularly pronounced during and after the withdrawal of U.S. troops. In some respect, the matter of national survival then became a question of whether or not military leadership could measure up to its historical role.

---

[1] President Thieu subsequently ordered the Minister of Defense to conduct an investigation to determine who was responsible for the demise of MR-2 and MR-1. The investigation was still under way when Saigon finally collapsed.

The successes and failures of this leadership are many. For the purpose of this monograph, I believe that the examples I have selected from among them amply illustrate the status of military leadership under President Thieu's regime, the most critical period of our history. These examples will be presented in the following order:

> The challenge of corruption.
> Leadership at the corps level.
> Leadership at the division level.
> Leadership at the province level.
> Leadership at the battalion level.

The Challenge of Corruption

The geographical area of Military Region 4 included the fertile delta formed by the Mekong River and its tributary, the Bassac. It was the rice bowl of South Vietnam and the most densely populated. The type of war being fought here was also different from other military regions; it was primarily a low-level, brushfire type of warfare. Pacification was the main concern of IV Corps, and the role of the territorial forces was, therefore, particularly important to its success. As a result, the RF and PF of MR-4 made up about 40% of the total territorial force strength of South Vietnam.

Despite their numerical strength, the RF and PF units of MR-4 performed very poorly. In early 1974, the JGS decided to conduct an investigation to determine why their combat capabilities were so low compared to those of the other three military regions. Six fact-finding parties dispatched by the J-3 Division, JGS, visited various parts of MR-4 and conducted a two-week investigation. Their final reports provided several indications of ineffective leadership and supervision. In general, the active combat strength of MR-4 RF and PF units was extremely low. On the average, each RF battalion had only from 250 to 300 men and some, only 120.

These facts were reported to President Thieu as part of a RF and PF improvement program the JGS was undertaking. He immediately detected the problem in MR-4 and directed a country-wide campaign to eliminate the infamous phenomenon of "ghost and ornament soldiers" particularly as it affected the territorial forces of MR-4.

The Vietnamese term "linh ma" (ghost soldier) applied to those servicemen, mostly private soldiers, who were no longer in service (dead, missing or deserters) but whose names still remained on the unit's control list and who, as if by magic, still signed the monthly payroll ledger to draw pay. Or their names might have been crossed out on the control list but still figured on the payroll ledger. The term "linh kieng" (ornament soldier) meant just that: those who did not serve the unit in any capacity other than being a kind of ornament such as office boys, domestic servants, and body guards, who were not authorized but were assigned to the unit. Most of them were sons of rich families who wanted to stay away from the hazards of combat. "Ornament soldiers" also included those who were authorized by the unit commander to continue their civilian business or trade and report to the unit only occasionally when their presence was required, such as during an inspection or unit strength audit.

The campaign against "ghost and ornament soldiers" in MR-4 was placed under the control of the IV Corps commander, Lt. Gen. Nguyen Vinh Nghi, who was assisted in this task by the JGS. After three months of work, there were many deficiencies surfaced and remedied.

It was discovered that the vice of "ghost and ornament soldiers" was real and widespread among MR-4 provinces. Three of the most common irregularities committed by unit commanders were: detaching soldiers from the unit without authorization; authorizing soldiers to stay at home and tend to their civilian business, and failure to remove the names of deserters from the unit's payroll. The roll-call strength of each RF company, as a result, was reduced to an average varying from 35 to 60.

After correcting payroll ledgers to match the true strength of all RF and PF units, the Administrative and Logistic Support Centers of MR-4 were able to return to the national treasury the amount of 600 million piasters, which represented what would have been paid out to all deserters and those missing-in-action.

Following this campaign, the vice of corruption that had debilitated the territorial forces of MR-4 was kept under control and there followed a marked improvement in the performance of territorial forces.

But corruption in MR-4 was not solely confined to the problem of "ghost and ornamental" soldiers among the territorial forces. It was in fact much more widespread and involved several province chiefs and a corps commander as well. As a result, an anticorruption campaign, which was initiated by religious factions and political opposition elements, soon turned into a strong movement. This movement at first demanded that President Thieu take action to purify the governmental apparatus. In subsequent developments, the movement expanded and publicly charged several high-ranking officials and general officers of corruption, including especially, Lt. Gen. Nguyen Vinh Nghi, IV Corps commander, Lt. Gen. Nguyen Van Toan, II Corps commander, and Lt. Gen. Dang Van Quang, Presidential Assistant for Security. To ease pressure, President Thieu temporarily removed Generals Nghi and Toan from command but chose to ignore the case concerning General Quang.[2] This anti-corruption movement reached its climax when President Thieu himself was publicly charged with corruption. This was a period during which President Thieu's authority was jeopardized and his integrity seriously questioned, a dark cloud indicating still darker days ahead.

Corruption was a topic much talked about in the RVNAF, particularly during the later stages of the war. Under President Diem's administration, little was heard about it. Then, there were only sporadic

---

[2] In terms of military professionalism, both Generals Nghi and Toan were good field commanders. General Nghi, in particular, excelled in staff work and exercised his command duties with methodical and calculated care. In March 1975, when serving as Commandant of the Infantry School, he volunteered to assist the III Corps commander in defending the southern provinces of MR-2. As to General Toan, he was appointed to replace General Ngo Dzu as II Corps commander at a time when MR-2 was heavily threatened by the enemy's 1972 Easter Offensive. He succeeded in defeating the enemy offensive in the Central Highlands and improving the situation in MR-2 thereafter. Subsequently serving as Armor commander and III Corps commander, General Toan was a courageous and professionally competent commander.

"misappropriations of funds" or purloin cases involving primarily personnel responsible for the management of unit funds. Pilfering and larceny were also committed by some involved in the management of military properties and materiels. By 1965, kickback and bribery were rumored to be practiced by some connected with personnel administration and logistics. But corruption did not become a subject of common discussion and concern until 1967 when the RVNAF initiated a program of development and improvement. It finally took the JGS concentrated effort during 1971 to curtail and counter corruption activities, which by now had become widespread in the RVNAF.

Within the RVNAF, corruption took many forms. As an example in financial management, irregularities were possible in several areas.

1. Misappropriations and thefts of funds by the unit financial officer or NCO. These usually occurred when the unit commander failed to exercise tight control.

2. Paying the soldiers less than what was due them. This could be a deliberate failure to return change, a reduction of food allowance or illicit deductions of pay.

3. Deliberate procrastination in paying out family allowances (for newlyweds, a new child, birth expenses), pay increases (new rank, seniority), death and missing-in-action gratuities, and delaying the paperwork involved in pension claims in order to extort some compensation from the beneficiaries.

4. Collusion between the unit commander and his finance officer to receive the pay of deserters and those deceased or missing-in-action (ghost soldiers).

5. Collusion between the unit commander and contractors or suppliers to divide the contract payments without delivery of services or supplies.

6. Extortion of money or receiving kickbacks from contractors. This was usually done by pre-arrangement (for kickbacks) or delaying payments upon completion of contracts.

In the area of personnel administration, corruption usually involved extortion or receiving compensation from those draftees or servicemen who wanted special treatment, promotions or preferred assignments.

1. Exemption from military service or deferment for reasons of health, family situation or profession.

2. Assignment to garrison duties in the Capital Military District, big cities or to non-combat duties such as administration, logistics, technical services, or to less hazardous duties.

3. Selection to attend technical service courses after basic infantry training or assignment to these services after graduation. This was most commonly sought by draftees and reserve officers in addition to non-hazardous duties or duties near a hometown.

4. Promotion and appointment to positions yielding material or financial benefits such as positions affording opportunities for corruption.

5. Freedom to run private business or performing a lucrative civilian job (ornament soldiers). This usually called for compensation and/or forfeiting military pay to the unit commander.

The area of logistics and procurement offered numerous possibilities for corruption.

1. Cutting back on allowances of certain supplies issued to servicemen such as food, clothing and commissary items.

2. Extorting money from servicemen or their dependents who requested military transportation for visiting purposes.

3. Misappropriation of military properties such as vehicles or construction materials for private use; theft and sale of military supplies such as gasoline, tires, batteries, medicine.

4. Extortion of payment from real estate owners in the requisition or derequisition of their lands and buildings.

5. Soliciting kickbacks from contractors in the award of contracts.

These forms of corruption that I have summarized represent only the most typical among innumerable others. It is indeed impossible to make an exhaustive listing of all forms of corruption, since in a country long at war there were myriad ways to make a profit for the corrupt-minded people. In short, as far as South Vietnam was concerned, corruption could be said to be a social vice generated by the war and by the insecure psychology which prevailed among those elements who cared little about the war or its outcome.

The impact of corruption on the RVNAF combat potential and troop morale was debilitating. Combat effectiveness was greatly reduced because the manpower which could otherwise be allotted to field units found its way into staffs and non-combat units. Troop morale, especially in combat units, was often low because no one was happy to fight and die when others were exempt from these dangers.

To combat corruption and remedy its damaging effects, the JGS initiated two major programs beginning in 1967. One of these programs was called "New Horizon," and the other was designed to improve and develop the RVNAF capabilities. Both programs complemented each other by combining anti-corruption with developmental activities. From the start, it was felt that these programs could not obtain positive and lasting results unless the corrupt elements were eliminated. The first step, therefore, consisted of screening the RVNAF ranks and identifying their corrupt members. This responsibility was given to the Inspector General Directorate. It was a difficult and extremely complex task, since corruption had become so sophisticated that there was seldom evidence or legal grounds for prosecution. In bribery, for example, there were countless ways of making and receiving payments for services rendered and it was always in the interest of both parties involved to keep the transaction between themselves. Detecting and gathering evidence on corruption, therefore, was extremely difficult. But the Inspector General Directorate did not feel discouraged by the magnitude of its task. After reorganizing and strengthening the inspection system at all levels, the Directorate kept its door open for all complaints, charges and information leading to the incrimination of corrupt officials. All servicemen were allowed to contact the directorate directly by letter or in person for that purpose, and their names were kept confidential to avoid reprisals. Beginning in 1971, our Armed Forces were also subjected to the investigative operations conducted by the Office of the Vice-President, which was in charge of fighting corruption, and the GVN Office of Control and Supervision (Giam Sat Vien). Corruption, therefore, had become the main target of coordinated and well-organized investigative activities.

These anti-corruption activities brought about substantial and sometimes spectacular results. Two of the most spectacular cases involved the 5th and 25th Infantry Divisions, where our Inspector General conducted a long and difficult investigation on charges of corruption involving "ghost and ornamental soldiers," bribery for promotions, contribution of money to unit commanders, and illicit use of military vehicles and construction materials. Since the charges involved general officers, the reports of the investigation were submitted to President Thieu for decisions and appropriate action. In the light of incriminating evidence, the President removed both division commanders, Brig. Gen. Le Van Tu and Brig. Gen. Tran Quang Lich, who were subsequently arrested and prosecuted by a military court.

The RVNAF anti-corruption activities conducted by the Inspector General Directorate also brought to light many other lesser cases of corruption. Those convicted were all punished appropriately. Punishments ranged from disciplinary confinement, removal from office, demotion and discharge to prosecution by a military court. In addition, efforts to purify the officer corps led to the discharge of a few generals and in excess of 4,000 field and company grade officers who were either found too old for their ranks or convicted of wrong doing.

Corruption was inevitable in a society ravaged by war. Debilitating as it was, the worst that corruption could do to South Vietnam was to weaken its combat capabilities and potential. The collapse of South Vietnam as a nation did not result from corruption but primarily from a change in strategy, which not only came too late but was also badly implemented, and the great reduction in logistic support.

Leadership at the Corps Level:
III and IV Corps During the Cambodian Incursion

At the request of the Cambodian government, on 23 May 1970, III Corps initiated Toan Thang, Phase 5 for the relief of Kompong Cham. *(Map 3)* Kompong Cham was the second largest city in Cambodia after Phnom Penh and the seat of the FANK MR-1 headquarters. The city's garrison consisted of four infantry battalions totalling approximately 1,000 men, supported by

Map 3 — The Relief of Kompong Cham (TOAN THANG 42, Phase V)

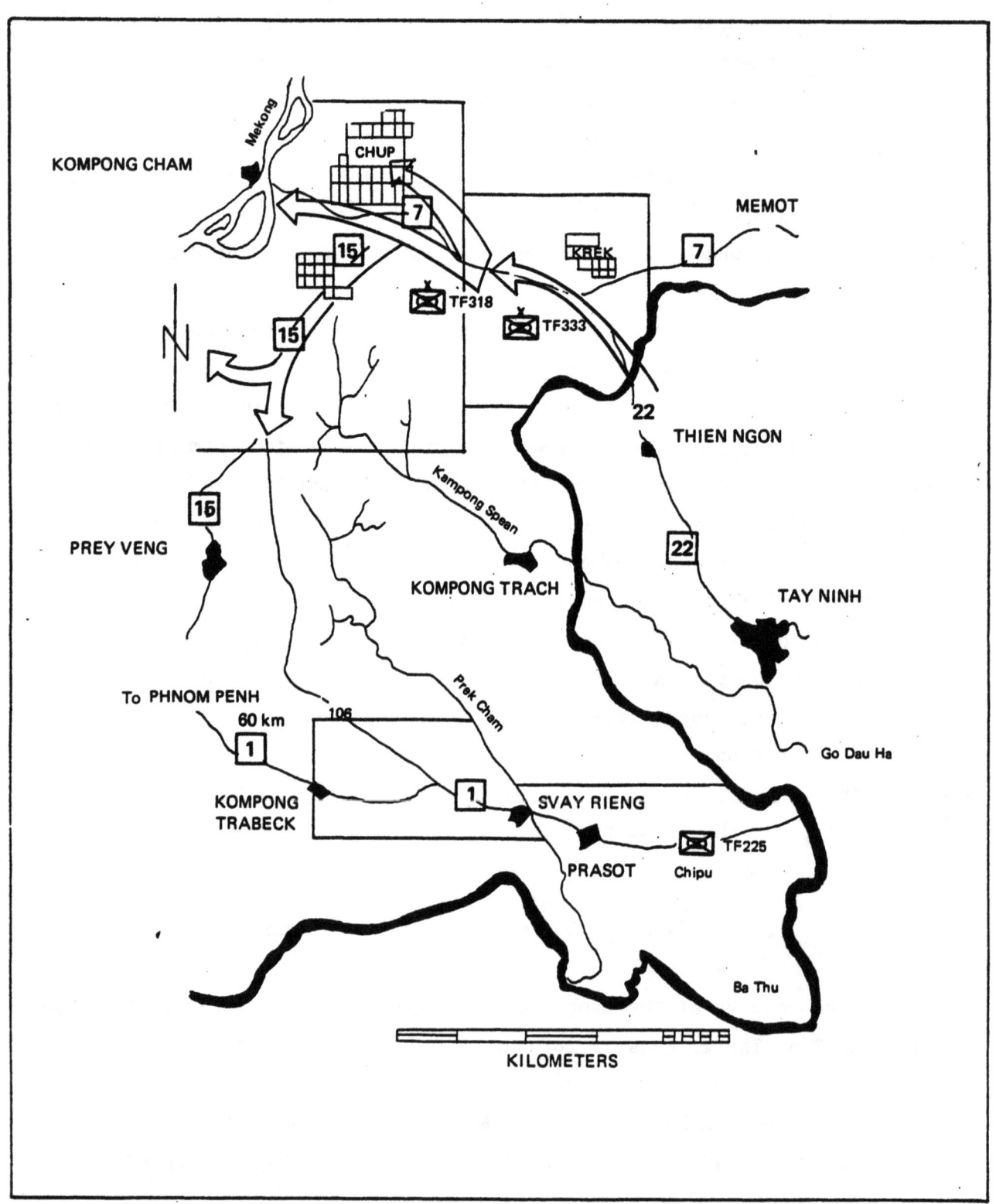

four pieces of 105-mm artillery with 1,000 rounds of ammunition. On 12 May 1970, units of the NVA 9th Division occupied the Chup plantation, east of Kompong Cham. Since that day, the city was constantly under enemy pressure. Both the city and its airfield were shelled day and night and the eastern part of the city was attacked several times by enemy sappers. Kompong Cham was practically isolated since the Mekong River, the major link between the city and Phnom Penh, and Route No. 7 had been interdicted by the enemy. The Cambodian forces defending the city suffered from low morale and shortages of food and ammunition.

To accomplish its mission III Corps formed two task forces, TF 318 and TF 333. Task Force 318 consisted of two Ranger battalions, the 18th Armored Cavalry Squadron, one 105-mm battery and one 155-mm battery; Task Force 333 was composed of two Ranger battalions, one airborne battalion, the 5th Armored Cavalry Squadron and two 105-mm batteries (-). From Krek and Prey Veng, the two ARVN task forces moved toward Kompong Cham along Routes 7 and 15 respectively; they were to converge in the vicinity of the Chup plantation. As soon as it moved out of Krek, the 7th Airborne Battalion of TF 333 clashed violently with the enemy. Supported by U.S. tactical air and gunships, this airborne battalion soon gained control of the situation, inflicting on the enemy 26 killed and 16 captured. The prisoners revealed they belonged to the 2d Battalion, 272d Regiment, 9th NVA Division. Task Force 318 also made heavy contact with the enemy on 25 May south of Route 7. The battle continued into the next day.

On 28 May, continuing its progress toward the Chup plantation, TF 318 clashed again with the enemy killing 73. The next day, 29 May, both TF 318 and TF 333 continued to battle elements of the NVA 9th Division in an area north of Chup.

On the morning of 1 June 1970, the Chup plantation was finally cleared of the enemy. Our forces continued searching for enemy caches in the area and expanded their activities northwestward in an effort to relieve pressure on the east of Kompong Cham.

Their mission accomplished, ARVN forces withdrew from Cambodia for rest and rehabilitation. Taking advantage of the ARVN withdrawal, the NVA 9th Division returned to the Chup plantation and again took Kompong

Cham under siege and initiated round-the-clock shelling. Once again, the city had to be relieved, and III Corps was assigned this task. For this second relief operation, III Corps employed three task forces and took six days to clear the enemy.

The cross-border operations that III Corps conducted in Cambodia produced important results. The enemy's heretofore inviolable sanctuaries had been severely disrupted and important quantities of weapons, ammunition, and foodstuff discovered and captured. Enemy forces were also driven back deeper inside Cambodia.

One of the important factors that contributed to these successes was the initiative enjoyed by our forces in an area which had long been under enemy control. The RVNAF also felt a certain pride in coming to the help of a neighbor country in distress. But the most important factor was excellent command and leadership, especially at the corps level.

The III Corps commander obviously had a talent for organization. He had judiciously tailored his forces to satisfy tactical requirements by creating armor-infantry task forces. Depending on the composition, III Corps might assign the command of each task force to a regimental commander, an armor squadron commander or the corps Ranger commander. This eventually ensured unity of command and tactical flexibility which brought out the best from each combat arm. Each task force was also a balanced combination of infantry, armor and artillery, generally comprising two or three infantry battalions (to include Ranger or airborne), an armored cavalry squadron and one or two artillery batteries. This combination afforded maneuver, shock and firepower in all operations.

During these operations, the task forces were always directly commanded by Lt. Gen. Do Cao Tri, the III Corps commander, assisted by an assistant for operations who was selected from among his division commanders. This arrangement for command and control provided for responsiveness and better support of all participating elements. General Tri was aboard his command ship all day and every day during these operations, making contacts, receiving reports, giving orders, and stimulating his unit commanders on the ground into action. The minute an objective was occupied, he arrived to survey the situation. When any of his units ran into difficulties or clashed violently with the enemy, he invariably landed on friendly positions, personally assisted the unit commander and encouraged the men. His ubiquitous presence on all battlefields greatly stimulated his troops and kept their morale and determination high. American reporters who accompanied General Tri into combat operations dubbed him "Vietnam's Patton." His combat prowess, personal courage and command ability became legendary and widely recognized. But occasionally, people thought that some of his gestures were ostentatious and calculated to convey an image of himself as a legendary hero. For example, in the battle for the Chup plantation, he landed the minute it was taken by our forces and inspected their positions. Then while the battle was still fiercely raging nearby, he took a dip in the plantation's swimming pool and quietly lunched in the plantation's clubhouse, as if nothing had happened. This was a peculiar trait of the man that few others possessed, including Maj. Gen. Nguyen Viet Thanh, the IV Corps commander, who was as courageous and almost as audacious.

Major General Thanh provides another fine example of effective military leadership amongst our senior officers. As IV Corps commander, he personally contributed to the success that his forces achieved during cross-border operations, especially Operation CUU LONG I. *(Map 4)*

On 2 May 1970, IV Corps initiated this operation in the Parrot's Beak area in coordination with III Corps. Major General Thanh personally commanded his forces which consisted of the 9th Division, the 5th Armored Cavalry Squadron and the 4th Ranger Group.

These units were organized into four infantry-armor task forces which moved out from Kien Tuong Province on three axes and progressed northward to link-up with III Corps forces in the Parrot's Beak. This operation was perhaps the largest conducted to date by the RVNAF and the best coordinated. All infantry and armor elements progressed rapidly on their assigned axes; they divided the objective into several areas in order to facilitate search and destroy activities. In addition to its organic artillery, IV Corps forces were supported by the U.S. 23d Artillery Group.

For two days, our forces made heavy contacts and inflicted severe losses on the enemy in human lives and weapons. On 5 May, IV Corps forces withdrew from the combined area of operation to prepare for the next phase. The results of this operation were impressive and indicated a high standard of military proficiency:

Map 4 — Operation CUU LONG 1, 2, 3, IV Corps

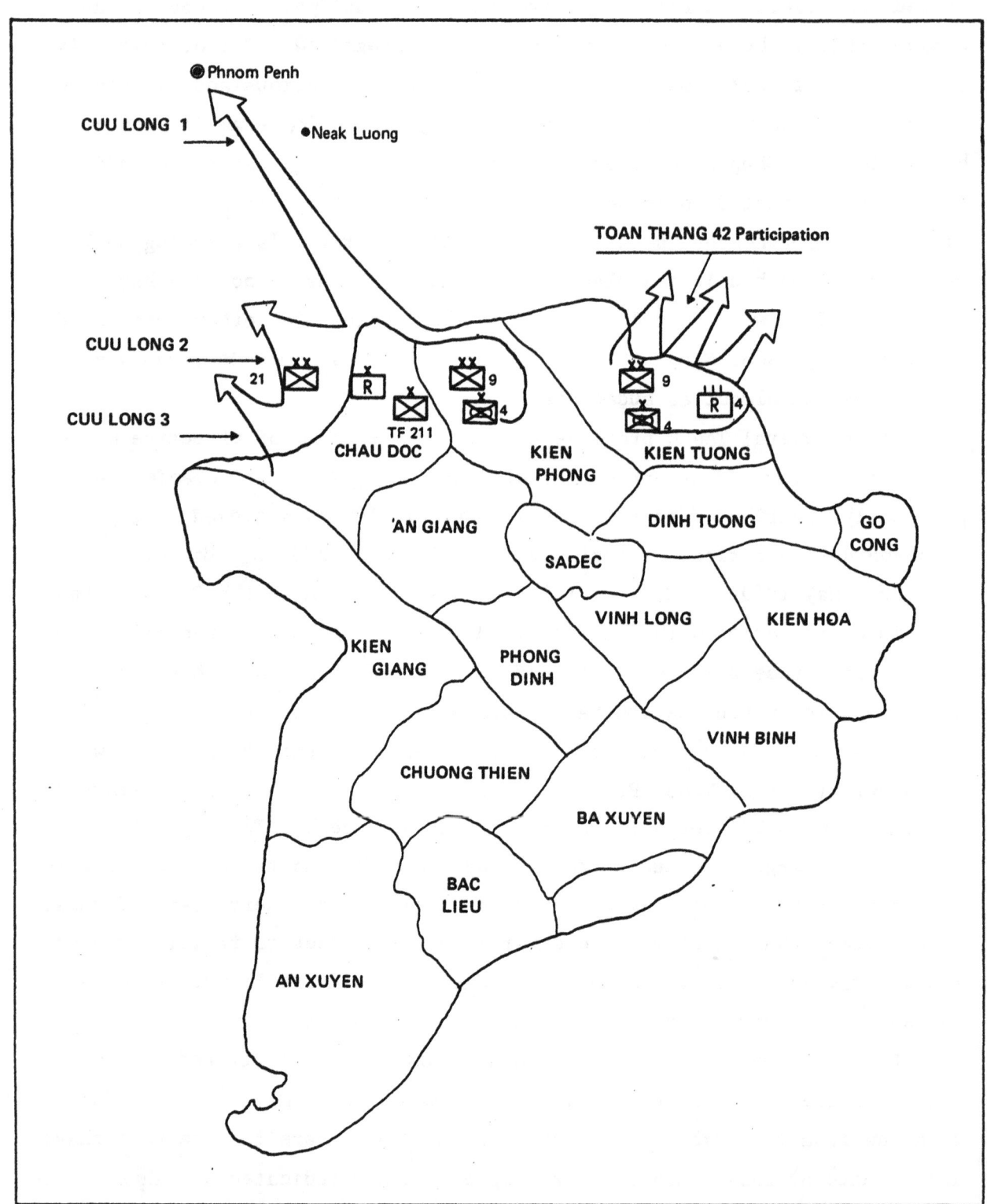

Friendly: 66 killed and 330 wounded

Enemy: 1,010 killed, 204 detained, and 19 rallied
1,166 individual weapons
160 crew-served weapons
100 tons of assorted ammunition seized and destroyed

This resounding success was directly attributed to IV Corps command and leadership. A poised and silent man, Major General Nguyen Viet Thanh had distinguished himself as a courageous and calm leader since the days when he commanded small units. He always studied the terrain, personally encouraged his men, and directed every major operation. As a result, he was greatly admired and respected by his subordinates. During the next phase of the operation, his command ship unfortunately collided with a U.S. Cobra gunship in bad weather. Both helicopters dropped to the ground in flames and Major General Thanh found tragic death.

About one year later, Lt. Gen. Do Cao Tri, III Corps commander, was also killed in a helicopter accident in Tay Ninh Province. The loss of two experienced and eminent corps commanders, both respectable leaders, in less than a year came as a great shock to the RVNAF. The war had definitely taken a heavy toll with this loss of two of the best military talents South Vietnam ever produced. The RVNAF death list during our extended war was certainly long with countless other young talents, perhaps not as celebrated as Generals Tri and Thanh, but equally courageous and devoted, who had sacrificed their lives so that our nation could survive. This was perhaps one reason why the RVNAF seemed to lack talented leaders at all levels, a void which became more acute when the nation had to face subsequently even bigger challenges such as the 1972 Easter offensive.

*Leadership at the Corps Level:
I Corps During the 1972 Easter Offensive*

The enemy initiated his 1972 Easter offensive by a frontal assault across the DMZ on 30 March. Within less than two days, all ARVN firebases north of the Cam Lo River fell into enemy hands. This blitzkrieg type action placed a new challenge on RVNAF leadership at all echelons.

On 2 April, the 56th Regiment, which defended Camp Carroll, surrendered after being encircled and heavily attacked several times by NVA infantry and artillery. Fifteen hundred men and 22 artillery pieces, to include four 175-mm guns, were captured by the enemy. Mai Loc Base, held by the marines, was evacuated shortly thereafter. Despite these initial setbacks, on the fourth day of the offensive, the 3d ARVN Division, which was responsible for the defense of Quang Tri Province, succeeded in establishing a firm defense line along the Cam Lo and Cua Viet Rivers, and temporarily stalled the NVA drive following orders issued by the JGS. (Map 5)

To strengthen I Corps's defenses, the JGS immediately reinforced it with one A1-H squadron, one marine brigade and three Ranger groups. All of these units were attached to the 3d Division by I Corps. As a result, the 3d Division found itself in command, control and support of two infantry regiments, two marine brigades, four Ranger groups, one armor brigade, and the territorial forces of Quang Tri Province. Neither the Ranger Tactical CP nor the Marine Division Tactical CP, which had been sent to I Corps by the JGS to assist the corps commander, were utilized or given a mission.

On 9 April, NVA forces launched a coordinated attack with major elements of the 304th and 308th Divisions and two armor regiments. This attack was driven back by ARVN forces, supported by strong U.S. tactical air, and the enemy suffered heavy losses, especially in armor vehicles. Because the terrain was flat and uncovered, most enemy tanks were easy targets for our tactical aircraft and infantry LAW antitank rockets.

In the meantime, farther south, the 1st ARVN Infantry Division effectively stopped all attempts by the NVA 324B Division and two other regiments to move toward Hue from A Shau Valley.

After repelling the enemy attack on 9 April, I Corps planned a counterattack to regain the lost territory in Quang Tri Province. An initial plan, which called for an attack across the Cua Viet River to retake the district of Gio Linh and the northern part of Quang Tri Province south of the DMZ, was discarded in favor of a drive westward. General Hoang Xuan Lam, the I Corps commander, decided to reestablish his former line of defense to the west by launching an all-out counterattack in that direction. Cam Lo, Carroll and Mai Loc were the major objectives to be retaken.

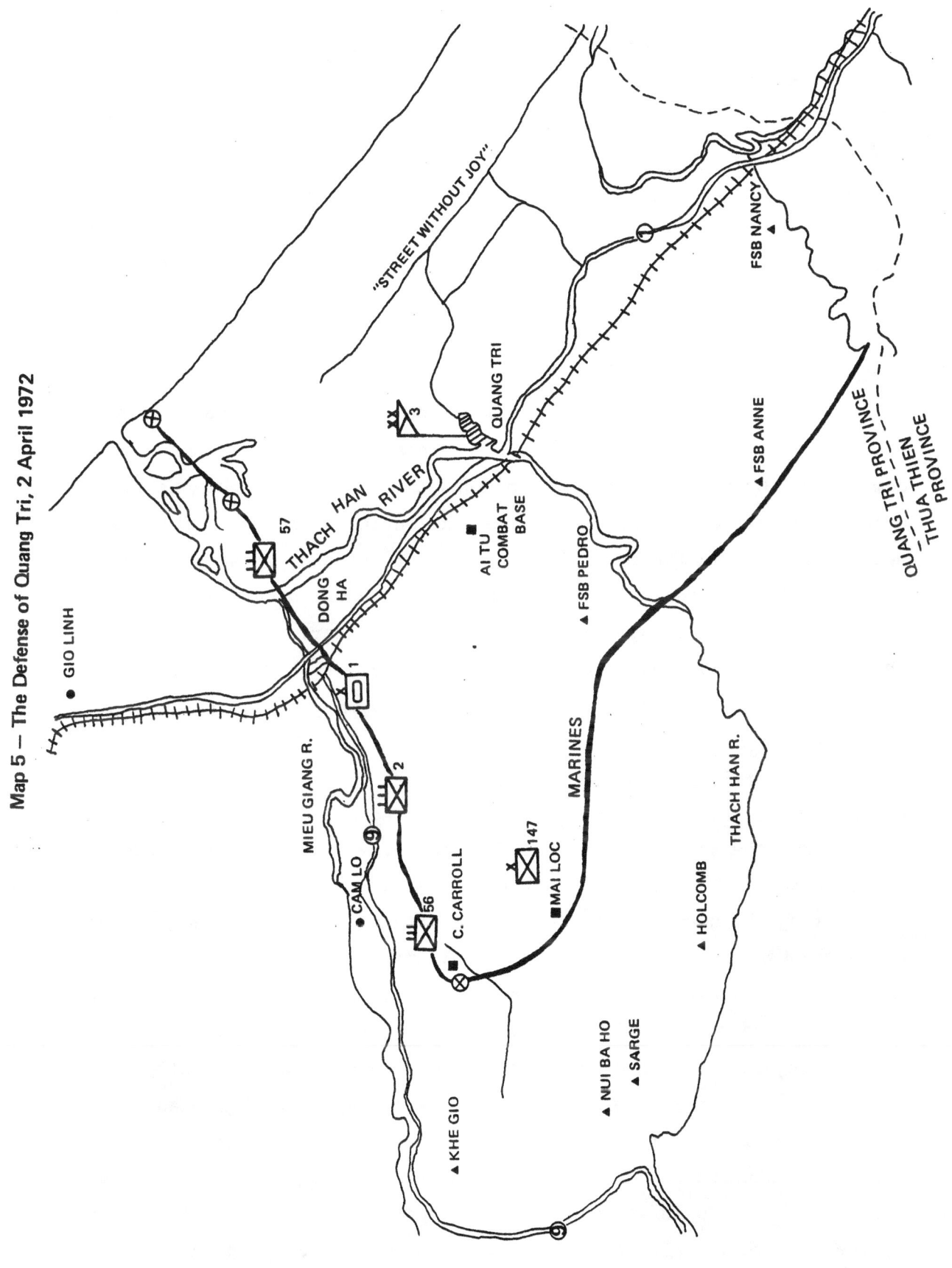
Map 5 — The Defense of Quang Tri, 2 April 1972

Orders for the counterattack were immediately relayed by the 3d Division commander to all of his subordinate units, but none of them seemed enthusiastic to move out. It was apparent that inadequate command and control and the low morale among units contributed to this general inertia and eventually, to the failure of the counterattack. Most unit commanders hid behind pretexts to justify their inaction: high losses or preoccupation with clearing activities in their own areas of responsibility. This general state of inertia lasted until the end of April, during which time no unit made any progress. The counterattack simply failed to materialize, and neither the I Corps commander nor the 3d Division commander seemed too concerned.

In addition to a loose and over-extended command and control system, I Corps performance was beset by the personal approach to command of its commander. General Lam usually bypassed the 3d Division commander, giving orders directly to the brigades under the latter's control. This was especially true in the case of the 1st Armor Brigade, whose commander was an armor officer, the same branch of service in which General Lam had received most of his experience as a junior officer. The authority of the 3d Division commander suffered accordingly, which eventually resulted in distrust and even insubordination among the many units attached to his command.

On 18 April, a second major enemy attack was driven against the ARVN defense line. All units on this line reported heavy contact with the enemy. But the attack was repelled three hours later by the forceful intervention of U.S. tactical air and B-52's.

During the week that followed this attack, the ARVN line of defense along the Cam Lo and Cua Viet Rivers collapsed for unwarranted reasons. It began when the 20th Tank Squadron left its positions on the Cua Viet line and moved south on Route QL-1 to destroy an enemy element which was threatening the axis of supply between Dong Ha and Quang Tri City. This was done without the commander concerned even reporting his plan of action to the 3d Division commander or to adjacent units on the line. Seeing that armor support was being redeployed and thinking that this was perhaps a withdrawal, ARVN infantry units left their positions and followed suit. By the time the 3d Division commander personally succeeded in stopping them, the Cua Viet line no longer existed. The ARVN defense line now shrank to the immediate vicinity of Quang Tri City.

As the first month of the offensive was drawing to its end, the enemy interdicted seven kilometers of Route QL-1 south of Quang Tri City. I Corps efforts to keep this road open ended in failure. Meanwhile, enemy preparations clearly indicated that another big attack was imminent.

On 30 April, the 3d Division commander summoned his subordinate commanders and briefed them on his plan to withdraw south of the Thach Han River and establish a new line of defense on the southern bank of this river with Ranger and infantry units, leaving the defense of Quang Tri City to a marine brigade. This redeployment of forces was designed to release enough armor strength for the clearing of Route QL-1 which continued to be interdicted. On orders, the units were to move out and take up new positions on the morning of 1 May.

General Hoang Xuan Lam was informed of this plan and appeared to approve by his silence. In any event, he neither confirmed his approval nor issued any instructions to the contrary. On the morning of 1 May, however, he called the 3d Division commander to inform him that the plan was not approved. He also instructed that all units were to hold their present positions "at all costs" and not to withdraw unless he personally approved.

General Lam was only reiterating the instructions he had just received from President Thieu in Saigon. But these orders immediately resulted in confusion and disorder the minute the 3d Division commander relayed them to his subrodinate units. In vain, he tried to countermand his own orders and issue new ones on the division command radio net. It was too late. Some units had already moved out, others pretended to be moving, and still others simply refused to comply with the new orders. One by one, ARVN units fell back from their original positions in disorder and it appeared that no force or orders could hold them back. Even the marine brigade, which was left to defend Quang Tri City, also followed suit without command authority. In utter despair, the 3d Division commander and his staff jumped aboard three armored personnel carriers and tried to catch up with the retreating column of ARVN troops. But on Route QL-1, the only lifeline to the rear, no movement was possible. It was clogged with vehicles, soldiers and refugees and all of them eventually became targets for the merciless poundings of enemy artillery. Despondent, the 3d Division commander and his staff returned to their CP in the Quang Tri Citadel and were later evacuated by U.S. helicopters.

The fall of Quang Tri City dealt a serious blow to the morale of ARVN troops and the local population. On 2 May, the people of Hue City began to flee south toward Da Nang, creating an incredible spectacle of frenzy and chaos. In the city itself, throngs of tattered and hungry troops roamed about menacingly like wild animals, ransacking houses, looting, and turning the place into a nightmare of terror and decadence.

When news of unruly Rangers ransacking and setting fire to the Dong Ba marketplace in Hue City reached President Thieu through a civilian source, he immediately summoned the National Security Council. In the face of this tragic situation, the council decided to remove General Hoang Xuan Lam from command of I Corps and appoint Maj. Gen. Ngo Quang Truong in his place. The appointment of General Truong, a southerner by origin, as I Corps commander was a departure from the normal practice of assigning that position to natives of Central Vietnam only.

The task that faced the new I Corps commander was monumental. He was expected not only to stabilize a chaotic situation of defeat but also to restore faith and confidence to the population and troops of MR-1. The first thing he did after assuming command was to strengthen I Corps command and control. Toward this goal, he established I Corps Forward at Hue with a select staff composed of able and combat-experienced officers. He placed particular emphasis on the development of a fire support coordination center to better employ all fire support resources available and a target acquisition element to judiciously exploit the enormous firepower provided by the U.S. Air Force and naval guns.

General Truong then initiated a new defense plan whose concept was simple but effective. It consisted of a clear-cut division of tasks and judicious assignment of responsibilities among subordinate units. Following this plan, he launched a special offensive by fire, called "Thunder Hurricane," which concentrated all types of conventional firepower available to include B-52's, on enemy targets in MR-1, especially those columns of enemy troops and supplies moving toward Hue. This was intended not only to destroy the enemy's offensive capabilities but also to buy time for the regrouping and refitting of those ARVN units retrieved from the Quang Tri debacle.

In a matter of just a few days, as if by miracle, the situation in MR-1 visibly improved and stabilized as General Truong's defense plan went into effect. And just as soon, stability on the frontlines brought back law and order to Hue. The city was cleared of all stray soldiers, who were given care and sent back to their units. The improvement in Hue was such that even though the danger of enemy attacks still persisted, the people who had fled the city began to return in increasing numbers. And soon Hue came alive again with the normal activities of a city in peace.

During May, the Airborne Division arrived in MR-1 as reinforcement after its brigades had been redeployed from Kontum and An Loc, regrouped and refitted. During the same month, marine units launched several limited attacks across their lines and inflicted heavy losses on the enemy. The enemy reacted by attacking our new defense line along the My Chanh River but to no avail. In the meantime, the battered units retrieved from the infamous debacle at Dong Ha and Quang Tri were refitted, retrained and reconditioned for combat by the end of June.

On the Armed Forces Day, 19 June 1972, President Thieu visited Hue and reviewed I Corps troops. On this occasion, he declared that the enemy Easter offensive was a complete failure and ordered the RVNAF to take back the lost territories within three months.

His orders were swiftly carried out by I Corps. On 28 June, it launched Operation LAM SON 72, a counteroffensive designed to retake Quang Tri. *(Map 6)* For this effort, I Corps employed both the Airborne and Marine Divisions. The Airborne Division conducted the major effort, attacking toward La Vang-Quang Tri on an axis west of Route QL-1. This effort was supported by the Marine Division, which attacked along Route No. 555 toward Trieu Phong. Meanwhile, west of Hue, the 1st Division held back the enemy who attempted to push toward the city in force.

Map 6 — I Corps Counteroffensive

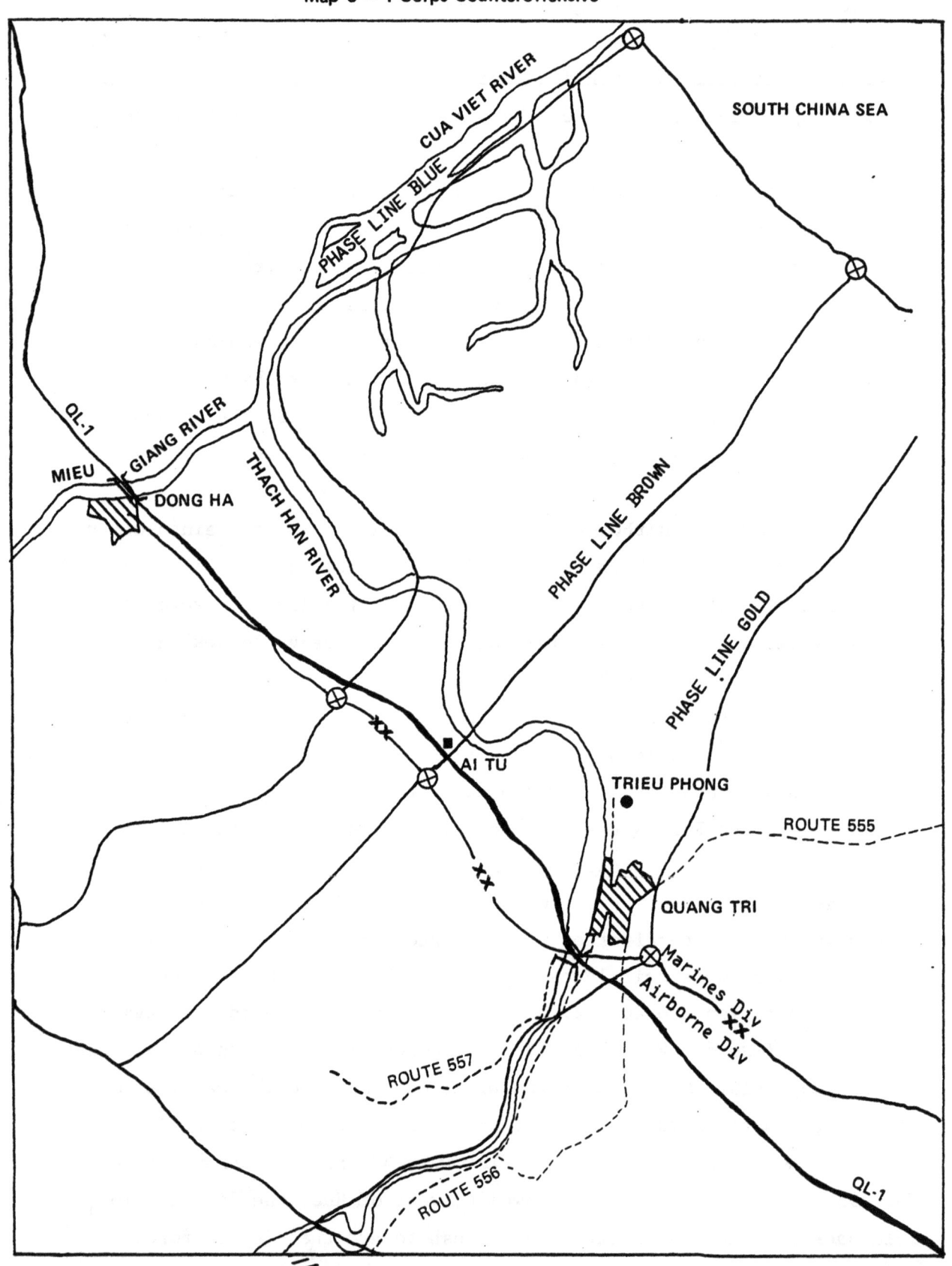

South of the Hai Van Pass, the rebuilt 3d Division assumed the defense of Da Nang and conducted limited offensive operations in Quang Nam Province while continuing its reorganization and retraining process. Farther south, the 2d Division searched and destroyed the enemy in Quang Tin and Quang Ngai Provinces.

The enemy's resistance in Quang Tri Province became heavier as I Corps forces moved nearer the Thach Han River. When the first airborne elements reached into the outskirts of Quang Tri City, the battle turned hellish. The enemy stuck to his positions and fought back in desperation, accurately employing concentrated artillery and mortar fire. As the fighting increased, the enemy moved in more reinforcements and by early September had assembled a force of six divisions in Quang Tri province alone.

In the face of this impasse, I Corps decided to switch units and the direction of attack, giving the Marine Division the primary effort. At the same time, frontline units were rotated and given a chance to rest and recuperate. To support the effort to reoccupy Quang Tri City, I Corps also launched secondary attacks to dilute enemy resistance. Eventually, softened by the massive and sustained firepower of B-52's, tactical air, artillery and naval gunfire, the enemy resistance weakened after severe losses. Finally, on 16 September 1975, the Marine Division took the Old Citadel and regained control of Quang Tri City.

A question arose frequently following the 1972 Easter offensive concerning the corps commander and the debacle at Quang Tri. If there had been a corps commander other than General Lam or if General Truong had been I Corps commander at that time, would the RVNAF have been able to hold the Cam Lo-Cua Viet Line? It is difficult to answer such a question since the circumstances of the debacle seemed to involve some intricacies that only the principals could clarify. One thing was clear, however. General Lam, as I Corps commander, certainly committed several blunders in his exercise of command and tactics.

An armor officer who had attended service schools in Vietnam and overseas, General Lam had once been an instructor and then director of our command and staff college. He had also climbed the military hierarchy as a unit commander. Therefore, he should have had sufficient professional competence and command ability to assume his role as corps commander with ease. In retrospect, however, his combat experience was limited to counterinsurgency warfare, and even as division commander, he had conducted only small unit operations for the purpose of maintaining territorial security. Therefore, when he was confronted with conventional warfare, which involved the coordinated employment of major units and fire support resources, he was at a loss. He could have overcome this shortcoming if he had practiced all he had learned and taught in school, especially modern warfare tactics and principles of leadership; but he had failed to remember his teachings.

His major failure was to overburden the 3d Division with a span of control so large that it was impossible for the division commander to exercise command effectively. With nine brigades, the division had virtually become a corps and under these circumstances, I Corps should have established additional divisional control headquarters by utilizing, for example, the Marine Division Tactical CP and the Ranger Tactical CP. When initiating his counterattack in April, the I Corps commander also failed to follow up and take appropriate action when units under the 3d Division procrastinated. This inertia obviously resulted from the lack of positive leadership and combat fatigue, which could have been remedied by a rotation of units. The command and control of the 3d Division was most difficult when the I Corps commander gave direct orders to the 1st Armor Brigade, maneuvering its units without informing the division commander. As a result, infantry units on line did not know why the 20th Tank Squadron suddenly left its positions. This confusion and poor communications also indicate why they left their positions to follow the armor south, resulting in the senseless loss of Cua Viet and Dong Ha. In general, under the command of General Lam, I Corps units seldom received clear-cut orders nor were they assigned well-defined responsibilities. This could be a result of the I Corps Staff's ineffectiveness or its not being properly directed and utilized. In any event, staff coordination was rarely effective when the commander himself was indecisive or failed to take appropriate action when required.

There was also another characteristic about General Lam which should be avoided by leaders at every level. He would not report bad news or was very slow to do so. When the enemy offensive first started, he failed to report accurately on the DMZ situation and as a result, the JGS had no way of knowing that it was a large-scale invasion. As chief of the JGS, I did not fully grasp the real situation until General Abrams, COMUSMACV, informed me of what was happening. My concern at the time was to hold the Cua Viet line, and I accordingly gave General Lam as much reinforcement as the JGS could afford. I also wanted to give him additional assistance by detaching a small staff to I Corps headquarters along with the general reserve units. But General Lam did not seem eager for this assistance; he almost ignored the presence of this staff, thinking that perhaps it was there to check on him. When the unruly Rangers set fire to the Dong Ba marketplace in Hue following the fall of Quang Tri, he did not report this either. I had the impression that he did not monitor the situation very closely or the developments in his area of responsibility.

Looking back on that difficult period of time, I can now see that it was perhaps unrealistic to expect perfection from a corps commander. The kind of training and experience, the influence of politics on officers of General Lam's generation and their very background perhaps did not contribute to the cultivation of military leadership required by the circumstances. The very nature of the war and our tasks at hand seemed to demand that a corps commander be not only a skilled administrator, a shrewd politician, a leader of men but also a good field commander well versed in both anti-insurgency and modern warfare tactics and able to employ the vast array of combat support assets in defense as well as in offense. Such omnipotent corps commanders were rare. But rare does not mean that the RVNAF did not have any.

One such corps commander was Lt. Gen. Ngo Quang Truong, a career airborne officer who served with the Airborne Division until he became its deputy commander. His combat exploits during this earlier period were many, but what distinguished him most was his innate and unique qualities as a leader of men. I don't think I need to dwell at length on his exploits because my discussions of the airborne tradition in the previous chapter should speak for themselves. Suffice it to say that Truong was one of the best commanders at every echelon the Airborne Division ever had. The only regrettable thing about his early career was that he did not have the opportunity to further his military schooling. Combat duties were so demanding that he hardly had time to attend the advanced courses designed for career officers like himself. However, this lack of advanced training certainly did not affect his military knowledge or professionalism. And he fully proved it when as I Corps commander, he successfully met the biggest challenge any ARVN field commander ever had to face. Not only did he restore morale and confidence to the troops and population of MR-1, he also quickly stabilized a despondent, chaotic situation and eventually retook that part of MR-1 territory most prized by the enemy. During the counteroffensive he was credited with several tactical initiatives that enabled I Corps forces to neutralize the NVA superiority in strength and artillery and finally destroy even the enemy's will and determination to resist. General Truong's success in accomplishing the almost impossible can be attributed to several factors but one thing was certain: his outstanding leadership had made him one of the most capable military leaders South Vietnam had ever produced.

Leadership at the Corps Level:
II Corps During the Redeployment from Kontum-Pleiku

The redeployment of II Corps forces from the Central Highlands in mid-March 1975 was perhaps a most ignominious example of leadership failure in the history of the RVNAF. It resulted in the tragic loss of this ARVN corps as a major combat force and eventually precipitated the chain of events leading to the final collapse of South Vietnam.

II Corps was under the command of Maj. Gen. Pham Van Phu, a presidential appointee like other corps commanders. Small and fragile, Phu did not look like a man for sustained or critical actions. His combat record, however, was good. He performed quite well during LAM SON 719 as commander of the 1st Infantry Division. As a junior officer serving in French Union forces, Phu had seen combat action at Dien Bien Phu. Just four months into his job as II Corps commander, he was about to face the biggest challenge of his military career.

On 14 March, 1976, two days after the loss of Ban Me Thuot City, President Thieu summoned General Phu to Cam Ranh for an exclusive meeting. During this meeting, the President ordered him to reoccupy Ban Me Thuot with II Corps forces still available. Since the 23d Division had been battered during the battle of Ban Me Thuot and the 22d Division was engaging the enemy at Binh Khe on Route 19, this implied that in order to carry out his mission, Phu had to withdraw all of his combat and support units from the Kontum-Pleiku area, bring them down to the coast, and launch a counterattack on Ban Me Thuot from there.

In the Kontum-Pleiku area, by that time, there remained one battalion of the 44th Regiment, five Ranger groups of three battalions each, one M-48 tank squadron, two 155-mm artillery battalions, one 175-mm artillery battalion, and Regional and Popular Forces units. In addition, there were logistic support units such as the 20th Combat Engineer Group, the 231st Direct Support Group, the Army and Air Force ammunition depot with 20,000 tons of ordnance in stock, a POL depot with a 45-day supply and a food and subsistence depot with a 60-day supply.

The withdrawal of this impressive force plus II Corps Headquarters and headquarters units looked like an impossible mission. Since the 6th Air Division at Pleiku possessed only marginal airlift capabilities, the withdrawal had to be effected by road. But which road? Of all major axes of communication which afforded II Corps a redeployment route toward the coast, none was free from enemy interdiction. The only road available was perhaps Interprovincial Route 7B; but it had not been in use for a long time, and its present condition remained unknown.

General Phu seemed to be sure of his choice when he selected Route 7B to move his forces. As he explained it during the Cam Ranh meeting, this route, despite its uncertain condition, offered the best chance of success because the enemy would never suspect that II Corps would use it. The withdrawal, therefore, had to be carried out swiftly to avoid enemy pursuit. (Map 7)

The idea of a surreptitious movement conceived by the II Corps commander to take the enemy by surprise appeared to dictate the way he was

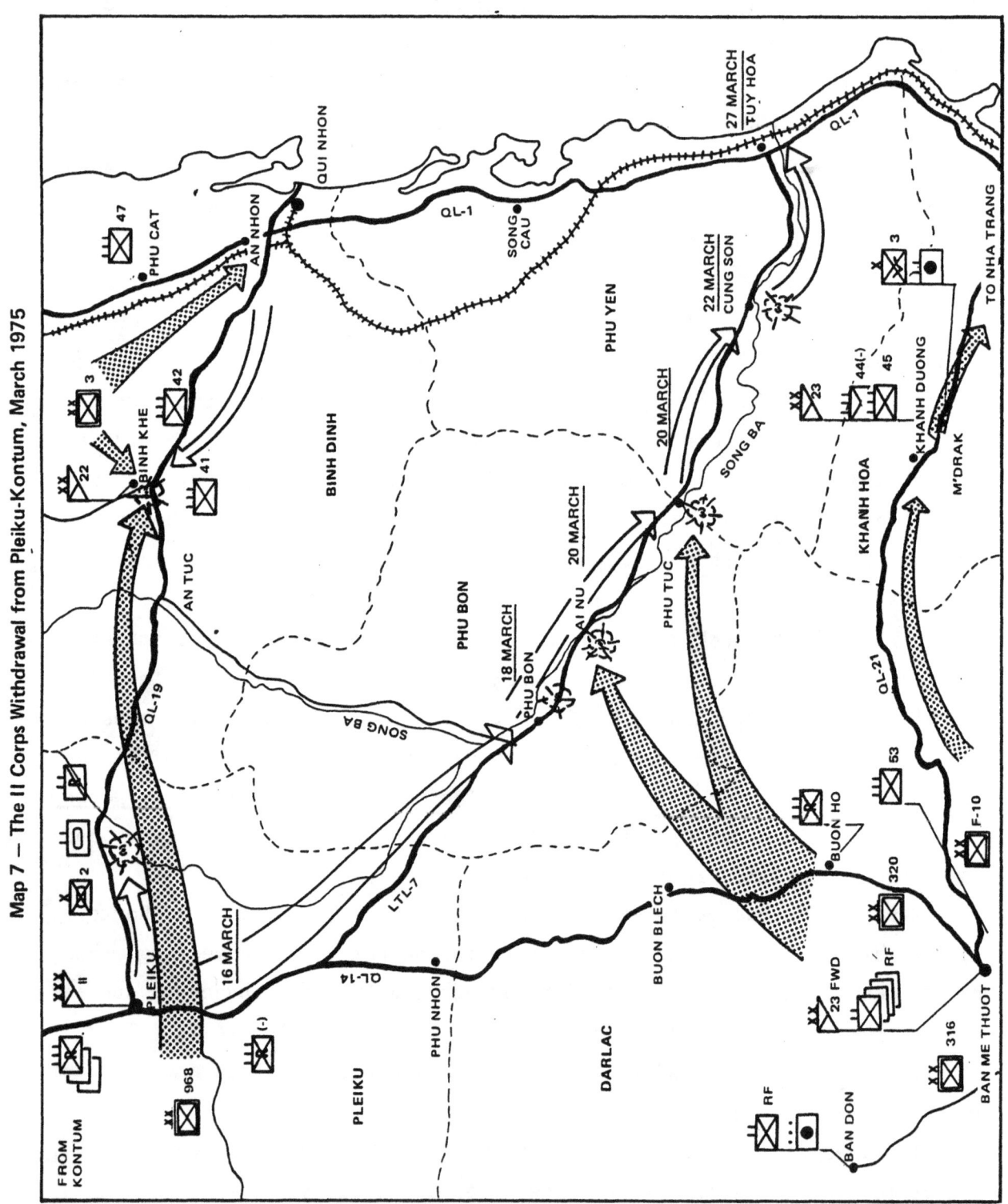

Map 7 – The II Corps Withdrawal from Pleiku-Kontum, March 1975

going to execute it. According to his chief of staff, Colonel Le Khac Ly, after he returned from the meeting late in the evening of the same day, General Phu convened a limited staff meeting during which he reported President Thieu's orders and issued his own for the redeployment. A general concept of movement was briefly discussed, and it was decided that Brig. Gen. Le Van Tat, the newly promoted Ranger commander and a protege of General Phu, would be in charge. Colonel Ly, the II Corps chief of staff, was made responsible for the corps staff and logistic units. The entire operation was to be supervised by Brig. Gen. Tran Van Cam, the assistant II Corps commander.

Since the movement involved thousands of troops, hundreds of vehicles, artillery units and other heavy equipment, a schedule was established to implement it in four consecutive days, beginning March 16. Each day, a convoy of 200-250 trucks would move out of Pleiku to be followed during the next three days by other convoys of similar strength and composition. Instructions were also given to the 20th Combat Engineer Group to precede the lead column to rehabilitate road and bridges as required. Armor elements were to be assigned to each convoy for its protection. Itinerary security was to be provided by local RF and PF units. Finally, two Ranger groups and an armor troop were to form the rear guard. They were to be the last units to move out of Pleiku on the morning of March 19.

The next day, March 15, while movement preparations were feverishly taking place, the II Corps commander flew out to Nha Trang with a few selected staff members, purportedly to establish a forward CP there. His assistant, General Cam, followed suit to Tuy Hoa on the coast, from where he was supposed to touch base with the advancing column. Neither ever came back on the scene again to supervise the troop movement.

Since the redeployment was conceived in secret and carried out in haste, II Corps command did not inform the province chiefs of Kontum, Pleiku and Phu Bon. Not until late at night March 17, the second day of the redeployment, were orders given to the three Ranger groups stationed in Kontum to fall back on Pleiku. Only then did the Kontum province chief, Colonel Phan Dinh Hung, learn about the troop movement. Hastily, he went along but was killed in an ambush halfway between Pleiku and Kontum.

On March 16, the first convoy moved out of Pleiku as planned. But no sooner had the last truck departed when news of the redeployment reached the city and made its impact felt throughout the population. Soon people began frantically to evacuate the city by every means of transportation available, even on foot, taking along with them whatever belongings they could manage to carry. Later, they were joined by refugees moving out of Kontum and mingling with the redeployed troops; they formed a long mass of humans and vehicles flowing along unexplored Route 7B.

The first two days, March 16 and March 17, went by without serious incidents. By the evening of March 18, II Corps Headquarters had reached Cheo Reo (Phu Bon) where a light CP was established. It was in this area that all the convoys of the past three days and the human mass of refugees were stuck. The advance toward the coast, still some 100 miles of uncertainty away, was impossible because the engineers had not completed in time a pontoon bridge across the Ea Pa river near the town.

During the night enemy troops, presumably from local units ordered to intercept the stalled column, began shelling and mounting ground attacks. The Cheo Reo airstrip, less than one mile from II Corps light CP, was overrun. Fighting continued into late evening of the next day, March 19. By this time, wounded soldiers and refugees alike were lying all around, unable to be evacuated. There was practically no control in the town. Some unruly Montagnard RF and PF troops began looting or broke ranks and ran away, creating a chaotic commotion among troops and refugees. The situation became increasingly serious as each waiting hour went by. It was then that from Nha Trang General Phu issued orders for Colonel Dong, commander of the 2d Armor Brigade, to take over command of the column.

The convoy moved out of Phu Bon the next day, March 20, but could only progress as far as Ca Lui, 15 miles away. Phu Tuc, farther down the road, had been overrun by the enemy. Still the convoy kept moving, fighting its way ahead. Air support was called at 1600 hours but unfortunately, a few bombs were dropped by error on the lead elements. Nearly an entire Ranger battalion became casualties. This fatal accident stalled the movement and increased confusion and chaos among the troops and refugees. In a frantic effort to seek cover and escape, several troops jumped into the river and were drowned. Other accidents added to the troubles and misery of the ill-fated convoy. At Ca Lui and Ai Nu, a river-crossing point, some tanks and vehicles were bogged down and stuck in quicksand while they tried to bypass the road.

At Cung Son, some 40 miles from Tuy Hoa, the convoy was compelled again to cross the Song Ba River to continue the last leg of the journey on Provincial Route 436 on the southern bank of the river. Up to this point, the convoy had been using Interprovincial Route 7B on the northern bank. However, beyond Cung Son, Route 7B had been mined extensively by the Korean forces during the time they manned an outpost here. But here again, the lack of river-crossing facilities stopped the moving column. A M4T6 pontoon bridge meanwhile had been brought to Tuy Hoa from Nha Trang, intended for the river-crossing at Cung Son. But it was impossible to move the bridge to Cung Son by road because of several enemy blocking positions. Efforts at clearing the road by RF units of Tuy Hoa Province were all defeated. Finally, the bridge was dismantled and carried piece by piece to Cung Son by CH-47 helicopters.

On March 22, at last the pontoon bridge was established, and the convoy crossed over onto Route 436 and proceeded cautiously toward Tuy Hoa. Because of the tremendous rush at the start, the pontoon soon collapsed, causing further losses in human lives and vehicles; but it was quickly repaired, and the battered column soon made it safely to the other side of the river.

If it had taken seven days and innumerable casualties for the column of redeployed troops and refugees to progress so far, the remaining and final leg of their odyssey was to be equally slow and even more hazardous. The distance was relatively short, but the blocking positions that the enemy had strewn along its course were hard to dislodge. No sooner had the lead element resumed its march when it was stalled immediately by enemy fire. Efforts at clearing enemy blocking positions were slow and difficult. The sector of Tuy Hoa had run out of reinforcement troops for the effort. So the whole column of humans and vehicles bogged down again on this side of the river. It was raining and cold. And the enemy relentlessly kept up his mortar bombardments and harassing fire. Because of rain and extremely bad weather, the air force was unable to provide close support. For its survival, the column had to rely on its own strength. Driven to desperation and out of a compassion for the people of their own lot, the gallant troops of the 34th Ranger Battalion (7th Ranger Group of the JGS general reserve) finally resolved to break through or die. Supported by the few remnant M-113's, they stormed ahead and systematically destroyed block after block. As soon as an enemy position was disposed of, the column rushed on, oblivious of all dangers ahead.

On March 27, the final blocking position was destroyed and the column at last moved on freely toward Tuy Hoa. It was 2100 hours when the first vehicles reached the city. No effort was ever made to keep a tally of the vehicles and people that finally made it to Tuy Hoa. How many vehicles and how many people of the original column had really survived the tragic journey, no one knew exactly. It was only known that approximately 300 vehicles, both military and civilian, later drove up to the fuel supply station set up by the 2d Logistic Command and asked for refueling. Also, approximately 5,000 people sought shelter at the makeshift refugee center at Tuy Hoa that night.

On the military side, the redeployment operation was deemed a tragic failure. Almost all units withdrawn from the Kontum-Pleiku area incurred losses amounting to 75% of their original strength.[3] But the gallant 34th Ranger Battalion, later dubbed "block destruction heroes" by the grateful refugees, lost only 50% of its strength. It was retained at Tuy Hoa for the defense of the city.

---

[3] According to an estimate by the chief of staff, II Corps, Colonel Le Khac Ly, 5,000 out of 20,000 logistic and support troops were finally retrieved.

Tactically, a retrograde movement is by far a most difficult maneuver. It is prone to disorder, chaos and disruption if command and control fail and if morale and discipline cannot be sustained. Hence, it requires a most minutious planning and a strong leadership at all echelons. The redeployment of II Corps troops from Kontum-Pleiku was not a retrograde operation in the accepted tactical sense. It was simply a scheduled movement of organized convoys with self-defense capabilities. The movement of the convoys was seriously impeded by the accruing and uncontrollable flow of refugees and civilian vehicles on the one hand and by road conditions and the lack of river-crossing facilities on the other. The 320th NVA Division, which was thrown in pursuit only after the enemy learned of the actual redeployment, could never have caught up with the column if river-crossing facilities had been provided in time and if the flow of refugees had been regulated by a tight control. The element of surprise could have worked. It had indeed for the first few days.

However well justified he was with his concept of tactical surprise, the II Corps Commander could not be spared the censure of having failed to establish a detailed plan with his staff and to exercise his direct control over the entire operation. Whatever planning he had done, it was limited, and only a few trusted subordinate commanders had contributed to it and knew about it. Staff work was entirely non-existent. Colonel Le Khac Ly, the chief of staff of II Corps, himself admitted he was totally in the dark. The commander of the 231st Direct Support Group in Pleiku recalled, in his own words, "I didn't know anything about redeployment orders. Not until an artillery unit nearby hastily assembled its men, equipment and dependents and loaded them on trucks, did I go out and inquire about it. I was briefly told, 'We're leaving town. Withdrawal orders. You'd better hurry.' So I hurried back to my unit, loaded some good equipment on trucks and took off after the artillery convoy. I had no time to destroy anything. I didn't even report my displacement to the 2d Logistics Command. It's supposed to be kept secret."

The II Corps commander's blind trust in his two trusted subordinates to carry out his orders had been misplaced. The entire redeployment

operation lacked unified and effective control from the start. General
Tat only looked after his Ranger troops. General Cam took no active part
in the whole process. His remote supervision was ineffective. The
overall control of the movement turned out to be actually exercised by
the II Corps chief of staff but only up to Phu Bon although he had not
been given this responsibility. The province chiefs of Phu Bon and Phu
Yen had failed to provide road security and protection. They were unable
to control their RF and PF units in performing this task. If they had,
if the itinerary had been protected and if river-crossing facilities had
been provided in time, the outcome of the redeployment would certainly
have been different. But excessive preoccupation with a false sense of
secrecy had precluded such vital pre-arrangements which could have looked
perfectly normal under the pretext of a road rehabilitation project. In
fact, such a project had been planned for some time by the JGS, to include
mine-clearing on the terminal stretch of LTL-7B from Cung Son to Tuy Hoa.

Finally, the failure was also one of leadership at all corps echelons.
Troops had not been informed about the operation and what had been expected
of them. Discipline had not been exercised, and constraints had not been
imposed in order to avoid disorder and chaos. In particular, they had
not been motivated enough to take on the difficult task of destroying
enemy blocks, the final obstacles on their way to survival. This failure
of leadership had resulted in a rout of strategic proportions. At least
75% of II Corps combat strength, to include the 23d Infantry Division,
Rangers, armor, artillery, engineer, and signal, had been tragically
expended within ten days. The operation intended to reoccupy Ban Me Thuot
never materialized simply because II Corps no longer had any combat troops.
And communist forces had taken the Central Highlands without a fight.

Leadership at the Division Level:
The 23d Division's Defense of Kontum

During the NVA Easter offensive of 1972, one of the major battles
was fought in the central highlands of Military Region 2. The enemy had
carefully planned and prepared and was determined to seize Kontum City.

To meet this challenge, the 23d ARVN Division was moved during early
May approximately 160 kilometers from Ban Me Thuot to Kontum. The
division commander, Colonel Ly Tong Ba, was given the mission of assuming
command of all ARVN forces in the area and reorganizing them for defense.
Even though he was a new and of course inexperienced division commander,
occupying the TOE position of a major general, Colonel Ba demonstrated
outstanding leadership ability during a most critical period.

The deployment of the 23d Division's units around Kontum City were
completed during the second week of May. This disposition was essentially a perimeter defense with ARVN infantry and armor units blocking
approaches from the north and northwest and territorial forces securing
the southern and southeastern approaches, facing the Dak Bla River.
The 44th Regiment was positioned astride Route QL-14, about 4 km northwest of Kontum, while the 45th Regiment defended the northern side of the
city and the 53d, on the northeastern side, protected Kontum airfield.
(Map 8)

At this time, the 23d Division was still untried in large-scale
combat and had yet to show that it was superior to its vanquished sister,
the 22d Division, which had been soundly defeated during the Dakto-Tan
Canh battle just three weeks earlier. But the division commander seemed
to make a big difference. Colonel Ba personally inspected the defense
perimeter with his staff, encouraged and provided guidance for his
troops on tactical details and demonstrated great care for them. The
defense, fire support and counterattack plans were coordinated and rehearsed daily, drawing from the painful lessons learned by the 22d Division. All units were given the opportunity to practice-fire the LAW
antitank rocket until their troops became confident. More importantly,
Colonel Ba's daily round of visits to his units greatly inspired his
subordinates, stimulated his commanders and instilled self-assurance
among divisional troops.

Finally, in the early morning of 14 May, the enemy began his
attack on Kontum. But the defending forces had been alerted since
midnight and were ready. ARVN intelligence in the meantime had been
able to detect every enemy movement and even knew the precise time of
the attack. Therefore, as the NVA troop and tank columns moved down

Map 8 — The Defense of Kontum

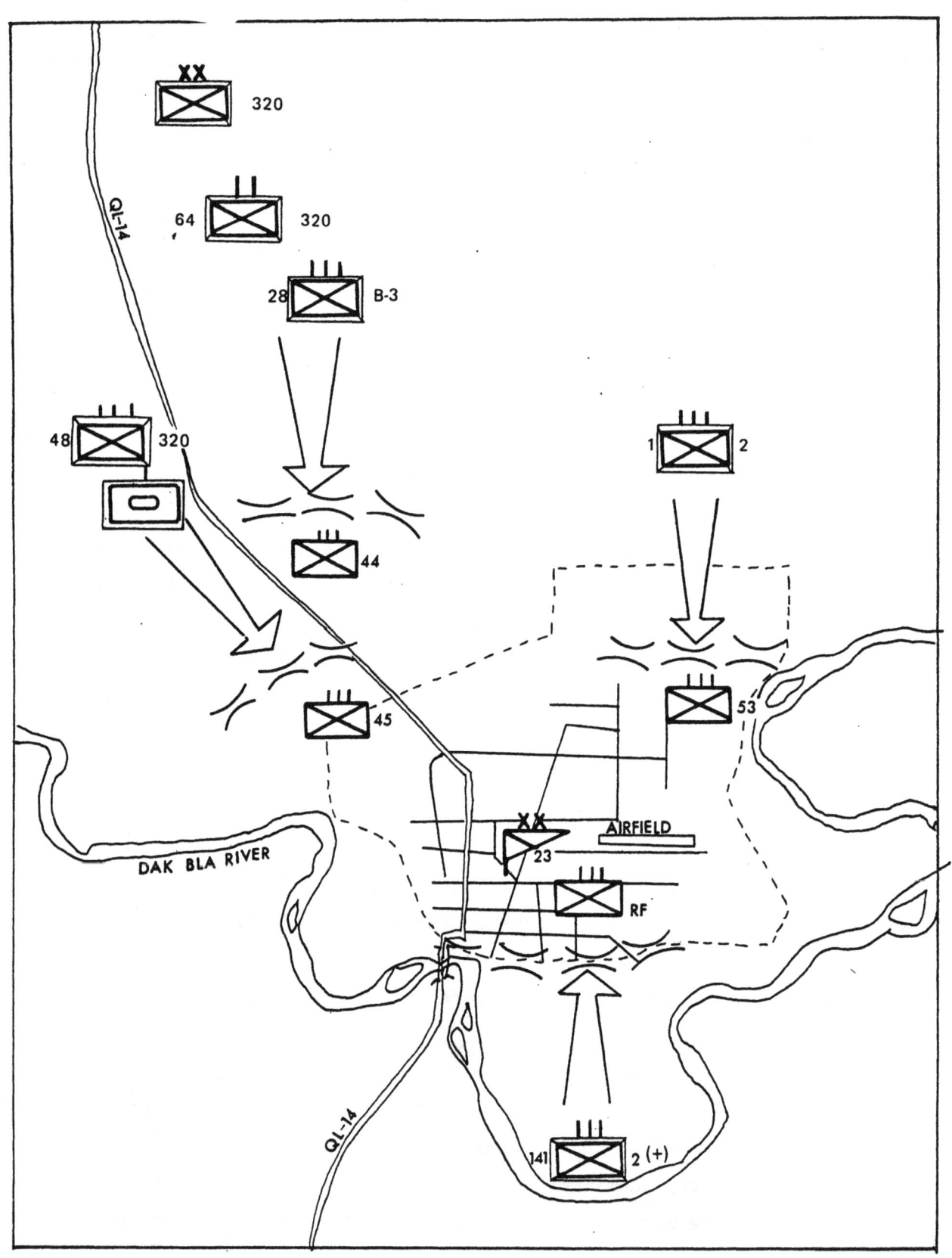

Route QL-14 toward Kontum, U.S. Cobra gunships, some of them armed with the new TOW missile, were already airborne from Pleiku. A total of four enemy regiments converged on the city. From the northwest the 48th and 64th Regiments of the NVA 320th Division and their tanks formed two columns advancing on both sides of Route QL-14. From the north, the 28th Regiment of the B-3 Front moved south against the 53d Regiment, while the 141st Regiment of the NVA 2d Division attacked territorial force positions along the Dak Bla River south of the city. Despite its combined force, this initial attack was quickly broken up after several leading enemy tanks were disabled by our artillery, LAW and TOW missiles. The reactions of friendly forces had been quick, decisive and successful, and the support of tactical air and gunships most effective. ARVN armored elements, although at greatly reduced strength and purposely kept in reserve, had quickly maneuvered to fill in gaps in the defense perimeter.

At nightfall however, the enemy renewed his attacks at an even stronger tempo against the 44th and 53d Regiments. Due to the confusion of night fighting, which hindered effective coordination, an enemy battalion succeeded in breaking through a gap between the two regiments. The situation became critical when this enemy unit enlarged the gap and exploited its gains with successive waves of mass assaults. Even our concentrated artillery fire failed to stop the assaults, and it looked like our defense would soon meet with disaster. As the situation was becoming more precarious by the minute, Colonel Ba and his staff worked feverishly on counter measures. The only effective way to turn back the massive penetration of enemy troops seemed to be the use of B-52 strikes, two of which had been pre-planned for the night. But the security margin required that ARVN forces be pulled back one hour earlier and to fill in this void, increased and sustained artillery fire would be necessary. Both ARVN regiments were instructed to hold in place and move back on order. This was a bold and risky move but there seemed to be no other alternative to save Kontum from falling before dawn.

The two B-52 strikes arrived on time as planned. As the rumbling stopped, a dreadful silence fell over the scene of fierce fighting. At dawn, ARVN search elements discovered hundreds of enemy bodies with their weapons scattered all around.

Success in this first contact gave the defenders of Kontum added confidence. They believed that enemy forces were no match for the devastating firepower of our air force and artillery in spite of their numerical superiority and powerful tanks. They had seen for themselves how the NVA "human wave" assault tactic was shattered by B-52 strikes. But Colonel Ba and his subordinate commanders realized that their first success had been close and that Kontum might well have been in serious jeopardy had it not been for the two timely B-52 strikes. In a post mortem examination of the results, Colonel Ba detected that there were several weaknesses in his defense. His units had been stretched too thinly over the defense perimeter, leaving gaps between them and making coordination difficult at limiting points. His staff had functioned well under stress, but some of its shortcomings needed improvement, particularly in the coordination of firepower. So he set about tightening his defense by reducing its perimeter and providing some depth by moving the 44th Regiment into a reserve position and replacing it with the 45th.

By the end of the week following the first push, all efforts by NVA forces to break into Kontum City had been defeated. Several times during this period, the enemy succeeded in breaking through our defense perimeter by forceful assaults against positions held by the 44th and 53d Regiments and penetrations between the 53d and 45th Regiments. The dent made into the defense line of the 53d Regiment on 20 May had been particularly serious and had warranted the commitment of M-41 tanks held by the division in reserve. Colonel Ba proved especially skillful in the maneuver of tanks, his own specialty for many years. His presence on the sites of battle also inspired his troops and helped them drive the enemy back.

His defense line having been stabilized and consolidated, Colonel Ba set about regaining some measure of initiative. With the support provided by U.S. tactical air and gunships, he launched several limited offensive operations in the areas north and northwest of the city within range of ARVN artillery. During these actions, scattered contacts were made as ARVN troops discovered additional evidence of heavy enemy casualties caused by B-52 strikes.

After ten days of holding actions to build up his forces, the enemy resumed his attack on Kontum on 25 May. As the 23d Division commander had accurately predicted, this attack had all the intensity and portent of a decisive, make or break effort. It had become imperative for the enemy to either achieve a quick victory or to withdraw his forces altogether for refitting. For one thing, the drenching monsoon was setting in over the Central Highlands, and its first effect was already being felt in the Kontum-Pleiku area.

The attack began in the early hours with artillery fire pounding all units of the 23d Division in and around Kontum City. The firing concentrated particularly on defense positions near the airfield and south of the city. At 0300, two enemy sapper battalions with the assistance of elements already in place began to infiltrate the southeastern positions held by territorial forces. They moved into an area near the airfield, occupied a school house, the Catholic Seminary and the Kontum diocesan office building. From the north and northeast, enemy infantry and tanks swarmed over and penetrated the city. Throughout the morning and into early afternoon, the division CP and ARVN artillery emplacements continually received incoming artillery and mortar fire. Fighting raged, and by late afternoon the enemy still held onto the areas he had penetrated. The enemy's ferocious artillery barrages during the day had taken a heavy toll of friendly forces. They also neutralized or destroyed a great number of our artillery pieces. The situation had become so bleak that a tactical emergency was declared for Kontum City in order to divert all available tactical air and gunships to the area for the day.

During the next day, 26 May, enemy indirect fire increased, and as coordinated attacks by enemy tanks and infantry pressed against the 53d Regiment from the north, pressure also mounted against territorial forces south of the city. With the support of Cobra gunships, an ARVN task force composed of one battalion of the 44th Regiment and eight tanks counterattacked and successfully contained an enemy penetration between the 45th and 53d Regiments. Still the enemy could not be dislodged from the positions he already held. The situation remained stable for the day, however. Meanwhile, the shortage of supplies had become critical for the defending forces, since the airfield was closed to fixed wing aircraft. The city's soccer field was used instead to accommodate CH-47 Chinooks hauling in emergency resupply and evacuating the seriously wounded. From the soccer field, VNAF helicopters shuttled supplies to the ARVN units north and northwest of the city. At nightfall, the NVA 64th Regiment attacked again, penetrating between the 53d and 45th Regiments and enveloping the latter. But again, scheduled B-52 strikes diverted on the forces attacking the 45th helped blunt this enemy attack.

In the early morning of the following day, 27 May, the enemy made a surprise thrust with two regiments and one tank company against the 44th Regiment, held in reserve in the city's hospital complex. Fierce fighting ensued in and around this area, resulting in a melee between enemy infantry and T-54 tanks on one side and ARVN troops and TOW missile-mounted gunships on the other. Due to the open terrain north of the hospital complex, enemy tanks were easy prey for the TOW missiles and ARVN LAW rockets. By late morning the enemy advance had been halted, but NVA infantry still held in the northernmost compound and continued to harass the airfield. From these and other positions across the northern part of the city, the enemy fanned out and formed pockets of resistance, particularly in those areas where friendly use of fire was limited. Despite all the efforts of ARVN troops and the firepower of U.S. tactical air and gunships and even the commitment of ARVN tanks held in reserve, it was difficult to dislodge the enemy from his positions. He seemed determined to dig in and exploit this precious foothold in the city.

To prevent further penetrations and consolidate his defense, Colonel Ba decided, with the approval of the II Corps commander, to tighten the perimeter again. This not only helped strengthen his defenses but also allowed for better use of B-52 strikes in close support. But by the night of the 28th, the situation remained critical. NVA forces were still entrenched in the hospital's northern compound, and the territorial forces were being engaged in house-to-house fighting in the southern area of the city where the enemy still held a school and a few houses near the airfield. By this time, however, the enemy was having serious problems with resupply. Air strikes had forced him to store his supplies at great distances from the city, and his transportation and communication lines were being disrupted. The critical situation around the city had also made friendly resupply and medical evacuation increasingly difficult, but airdrops and CH-47 Chinooks from Pleiku nearby responded adequately to emergency requirements.

The enemy's continued attrition by airstrikes and gunships finally allowed ARVN forces to counterattack and regain the initiative. To dislodge the enemy, they had to resort to bunker-to-bunker fighting and hand grenades. Shortly before noon on 30 May, ARVN forces had regained control of the entire hospital complex, and although there still remained other scattered pockets of resistance in the northeastern area, the city was clearly out of danger. In the afternoon, President Nguyen Van Thieu flew into Kontum City despite sporadic rocket and mortar fire. He praised the endurance and fighting spirit of all ARVN forces defending the city, and there, on the battlefield, he pinned the brigadier general star on Colonel Ly Tong Ba, the defender of Kontum, for "special frontline merits."

Then slowly but surely, during the remainder of the day all the enemy positions were taken back. By midday of 31 May, the battle was practically over, since NVA main forces had retreated. Thousands of NVA bodies lay scattered over the battlefield with dozens of T-54 tanks, some intact, but most reduced to charred hulks awkwardly perched among ruins. The enemy's final attempt to take Kontum had ended in utter defeat.

During the battle of Kontum, the 23d Division commander had proved to be a resourceful commander and fine troop leader. Realizing that unity of command was essential for his task, he had asked for his own regiments to be brought into Kontum to replace the Ranger groups. This greatly facilitated his exercise of command and control. Then he provided detailed guidance for his regimental commanders on defense and counterattack plans and ensured that divisional troops practiced the effective use of antitank weapons. His daily rounds of visits to all defending units were also an important factor that contributed to the high combat spirit of his troops. After the enemy's first attack, the 23d Division commander had the good initiative to reduce and consolidate the city's defense perimeter although the enemy had been driven back. The enemy

had several times attempted to break through this perimeter but failed
because Colonel Ba skillfully used and personally commanded his armor
and infantry reserve forces to counterattack and effectively seal the
breaches. He again proved to be resourceful when he decided to further
reduce the defense perimeter after the second attack when the situation
had become critical. But most importantly, he had fought hand in hand
with his troops and shared dangers and difficulties with them. His
fine and strong leadership made it possible for the 23d Division to hold
and win the final battle for Kontum.

The Leadership of the Province Chiefs of Binh Dinh, Thua Thien and Khanh Hoa

The years 1969, 1970, and 1971 were the best years for South Vietnam during President Thieu's administration. The country was not only militarily secure, it was well on its way toward full-scale development as a result of spectacular achievements in pacification. This was the main reason why the GVN embarked on an ambitious four-year plan beginning in 1972, setting high goals for community defense and local development.

The success of pacification during this period naturally depended on province chiefs, most of whom were also military officers. With a few exceptions, they had contributed a great deal to this success. One reason for this was their high caliber, the result of careful selection.

The position of province chief was unique among the assignments that a field grade officer might have during his career. It was also a unique challenge that taxed his leadership to the extreme of its requirements. Because of the dual aspect of the war, a province chief had to be first and foremost a good tactical commander, well versed not only in counter-insurgency tactics but also in modern warfare. More often than not, he was required to participate in combined operations with major ARVN and U.S. units, and to earn the respect of these units commanders, he had to show he was an equal. The command and control of RF and PF units in a province was not an easy exercise. Not only were they scattered throughout the province, their aggregated strength sometimes exceeded that of an infantry division.

To govern a province effectively, a province chief had to be an able administrator also. He had to supervise a large bureaucracy, prepare and execute the provincial budget, regulate trade and commerce, and protect national resources under his custody. With the advent of pacification, he had to plan for and meet the objectives set forth for security and development, and this required his involvement in countless programs and projects whose implementation needed his constant supervision and guidance. Toward the people he governed, a province chief had to show he was a sensitive leader who listened to their demands and grievances, cared for their lives and welfare, and responded to their aspirations.

Finally, in the exercise of his duties, a province chief was usually required to be a public-relations man and a politician. He had to receive guests, brief visitors and escort dignitaries on tours. He had to juggle among political factions and endeavor not to antagonize any. Whatever his creed, he had to show equal regard for all religious groups and sects, whether they be Roman Catholics, Protestants, Buddhists, Cao Dai or Hoa Hao. In brief, a province chief had to be many things combined in one.

As a result the province chief was overburdened by his responsibilities. No matter how devoted he was, he simply could not perform all of his duties effectively. So large were the province chief's responsibilities that many had suggested that they be divided between a province chief, who would be solely in charge of administration and development, and a sector commander, who would be responsible for security and operational matters. Perhaps this arrangement would have been more responsive to the dual aspect of the war.

The three examples that I have selected emphasize a simple fact of life: that if there are good men, there are also bad ones, and this is also true of South Vietnamese province chiefs. But by and large, the military officers who also served as province chiefs had acquitted themselves of their role in a most commendable way.

The first example involves a Lt. Col. in the J-5 Division of the JGS, as a plans officer he proved to be an excellent staff officer. With an analytical mind and a talent for organization, he performed his staff duties extremely well. He was also combat experienced, having served successfully as chief of staff of Thua Thien Sector and chief of staff of an infantry regiment. So when he was appointed province chief of Binh Dinh, everybody expected that he would be a successful one by virtue of his ability and experience. Binh Dinh was one of the most difficult provinces of MR-2. The enemy pressure here was strong and the majority of the local population had been subjected to communist influence for a long time. But the provincial territorial forces under the province chief's control were also strong; there were in fact more RF and PF units here than in any other province. During the first few months in office this officer did quite well. Subsequently, however, there arose charges that he allowed his wife to run a gambling den and favored his relatives with many commercial and business privileges to the detriment of local businessmen. There were also reports of selling and buying lucrative positions in the provincial military and administrative systems. These abuses of power were investigated by the GVN Office of Control and Supervision. The colonel was removed from office pending investigation and possible prosecution. Subsequently, his promotion was delayed for several years, and he was finally assigned to an immaterial job in MR-4. This was a typical example of a capable military officer who would otherwise have succeeded in his duties of province chief had he not been tempted by money and material rewards. This type of weakness in character was often impossible to detect during the selection process for responsible positions.

Not all province chiefs were corrupt, however. There were many who distinguished themselves not only by their integrity but also by their devotedness and fine performance. One among them was Colonel Le Van Than, province chief of Thua Thien and mayor of Hue City, who once served as deputy director of the Joint Operations Center, JGS. At first he had a special challenge since he was a native of North Vietnam and not expected by some to fit well into a slot usually earmarked for natives of Central Vietnam. But Colonel Than proved to be an exception to this rule, and he became one of our finest and most successful province chiefs. A resourceful, hard-working, and highly devoted officer, he learned very quickly the intricacies of local politics and managed to carry out his duties with distinction without offending any political faction. That he had succeeded where others might have failed could be attributed to his adroitness and flexibility, the qualities found only in a shrewd politician. But he was also an excellent tactical commander as well. In close cooperation with the U.S. 101st Airborne Division and ARVN units, Colonel Than greatly improved security in his province and achieved outstanding results in pacification and development. Because of his distinguished service, he was subsequently placed in command of the 1st ARVN Division and promoted to brigadier general.

Many other province chiefs were less successful than Colonel Than. In fact, several among them produced only medium results in their jobs; for example, Lt. Col. Le Khanh, province chief of Khanh Hoa. Originally a Special Forces officer, Colonel Khanh was a man of tact and gentle manners. Perhaps because of this, he remained province chief for several years. His performance was just about average, and he served without distinction, although Khanh Hoa was a relatively secure province compared to others. Despite this, he continued his career as province chief for several more years, being subsequently nominated province chief of Kien Tuong and then Kien Giang. People said he was a man of luck. In retrospect, however, it is clearly obvious that Colonel Khanh was completely loyal to his superiors, dependable, conscientious and devoted in the performance of his duties but did not possess the strong leadership ability required for the more critical areas of South Vietnam.

A Battalion Commander: Tong Le Chan

Tong Le Chan was a Ranger border camp located in the middle of a Communist-controlled area in northwestern Military Region 3. Manned by the 92d Ranger Battalion, its mission was to interdict enemy communications from War Zone C north of Tay Ninh to either Binh Long, Binh Duong or War Zone D. The location of this base caused the enemy many difficulties because he was compelled to use long detours. Therefore, he initiated a siege of Tong Le Chan Base on 25 March 1973 in an attempt to force its evacuation. As a result all ground supply routes used by the base were interdicted, and our patrols made increasing contacts. The small airstrip near the base also came under constant enemy indirect fire. Helicopters found it hazardous to bring supplies to the base because of the enemy's antiaircraft weapons around it. Although airdrops kept the base resupplied, a substantial part of them missed and fell into enemy hands, to include food and ammunition. During the 16 weeks that followed, the enemy conducted a total of 300 shellings against the base, firing more than 10,000 assorted rounds of artillery. He also attacked the base eleven times with infantry and nine times with sappers. As pressure on the base mounted, the enemy increased his propaganda campaign, promising a way out for the entire garrison. By July 1973, most of the defending forces on the base had become disabled either by wounds or illnesses with 30 dead and seriously wounded. But the 92d Ranger Battalion fought on courageously and was determined to hold this base. But the rainy season was approaching, and the unit had fought long enough under extremely harsh conditions. Orders were, therefore, given for defending forces to fall back on An Loc. The evacuation was well planned and well executed. After destroying all of its heavy equipment, the battalion withdrew safely to An Loc.

There was no doubt that the 92d Ranger Battalion was a tightly-knit unit and well led at every echelon. Under the command of Lt. Col. Ngon, this battalion had fought valiantly and cohesively from the beginning of the siege until it was ordered to withdraw. During these long months of heavy pressure and hardship, the battalion never revealed any signs of weakness or yielding to enemy threats. Despite constant enemy shellings and attacks, its disposition for defense never broke down. On the contrary, the will to resist among the men seemed to grow stronger as the fighting became harder. This showed how well the defense had been planned and how strong Colonel Ngon's leadership had been.

A combat-experienced and courageous commander, Colonel Ngon also proved he was an excellent leader. He kept the morale of his men high even during the most desperate moments by showing constant concern for their condition and welfare. He saw to it that the wounded were well cared for, stimulated the able-bodied to fight on and visited them around the clock at their positions with words of encouragement or praise. When supplies ran low, he shared the privations with his men and above all, never showed any concern for his own well-being or life. Inspired by his marvelous leadership, the men of the 92d Ranger Battalion enthusiastically responded to his orders and effectively fought on as a cohesive unit. This exploit was to remain one of the most extolled examples of leadership in the Army of the Republic of Vietnam.

CHAPTER V

Summary and Conclusions

Military leadership was not a continuous Vietnamese tradition. Interrupted and lost during the century of French domination, this tradition was not born again until we regained our national independence.

Traditional Vietnamese society under French colonialism regarded the military as a lowly profession, which it associated with servility and collaborationism. As a menial group serving the occupation forces, the Vietnamese military did not even count as a social class; they were the outcast of society. This contempt for the military, which reflected the passive opposition of the Vietnamese people toward French rule, still lingered until the Vietnamese National Army was formed in 1950. Even Bao Dai meekly admitted this as a fact.

The French presence, therefore, not only served to perpetuate this negative attitude; it also accounted for the complete void in military leadership upon their departure. This was a legacy whose consequences South Vietnam had to bear during its formative years. And the product of that legacy—the infant Vietnamese Armed Forces—grew up and matured only after severing all ties with it.

The examples of RVNAF leadership that I have discussed are superimposed on the political, military, and social background of South Vietnam with which they are intricately entwined. This serves to bring out a point of fact: that military leadership in South Vietnam was shaped by the stresses that affected the nation and that its requirements depended on the political dictates of each major historical period.

During the post-colonial period, which lasted up to 1954, French influence was still predominant as South Vietnam struggled to become an independent nation. Vietnamese military leadership, in a purely nationalistic sense, was non-existent during this transitory period. The 5-year old Vietnamese National Armed Forces did not have a command and control system of their own. Neither did they possess a clear-cut identity. They were but an appendage of the French Expeditionary Corps under whose leadership they fought against the Viet Minh without much conviction.

High-ranking Vietnamese officers who served in key staff and command positions were all graduates of French military schools, or reassigned from French Union Forces. Several among them even had French nationality and comported themselves in the manner of French colonels from whom they had inherited the major traits of leadership: haughtiness, authoritativeness, and lack of empathy.

But it was during this period that a new generation of Vietnamese officers was born. Those were the graduates of the first classes of reserve officer schools, Nam Dinh and Thu Duc, and the Dalat Inter-Arms Military School. They were to become the backbone of military leadership in the RVNAF. In fact, most of the higher-level commanders discussed in the examples, and Thieu and Ky, belonged to this group. The most distinctive traits that set this emerging generation of leaders apart from their predecessors were: strong anti-French feelings, political awareness, and dedication to the national cause.

The First Republic, which was established in 1955 under President Ngo Dinh Diem, saw the emergence of the Republic of Vietnam Armed Forces as an autonomous and truly nationalistic entity after command and control were wrested back from the departing French Forces. With direct military aid and advisory assistance from the United States, the RVNAF gradually developed into a modern, conventional, tri-service military force. For the first time, Vietnamese officers and NCOs were exposed to new methods of training, a new military doctrine and a new approach to leadership. Some found these innovations too exacting, but most agreed that they worked better and were more consistent with the national objectives.

The challenge posed by dissident religious sects and the Binh Xuyen provided the RVNAF with the first test of military leadership.

Even though some commanders came out of it with high honors, the challenge was localized and deemed not important enough to be a full measure of RVNAF leadership.

As the RVNAF reorganized and consolidated their training base, the selection of officer and NCO candidates become more rigorous, and more emphasis was placed on unit training. The creation of infantry divisions provided a good framework for this type of training and an excellent proving ground to foster military leadership, especially at the battalion level and above.

Military authority, however, was concentrated in the presidency despite the existence of the Joint General Staff. The President exercised this authority either directly or through the Ministry of Defense. Promotions and appointments, especially to key command positions, all came from the palace. As the regime sought to consolidate itself through a monolithic political party, cronyism became the practice of personnel selection, which was based not so much on professional competence as on personal loyalty and political affiliation. Cronyism eventually turned the most trusted but less competent officers of the regime into courtiers who fawned their way up the military hierarchy and created dissension among the RVNAF ranks.

For all its flaws, the Diem administration must be credited with strong national leadership and laudable achievements. It restored national authority, developed the economy, reorganized the armed forces and turned South Vietnam into a nation of world stature in Southeast Asia. To combat communist insurgency activities, which increasingly threatened the nation's survival since 1959, the GVN instituted an antithetic national idelogy culminating in the Strategic Hamlet program. Despite criticisms and excesses, this strategic concept was sound enough to provide the foundation for pacification and development in the years ahead.

As an individual, President Diem was widely recognized as a deeply patriotic, highly ethical, honest, and rather austere national leader who abhorred luxury and devoted all of his time and energy to state affairs. The "eminence grise" of the regime, however, was his younger brother, Mr. Nhu. A silent and meditative scholar, Mr. Nhu distinguished himself by his vast knowledge, sharp intelligence and innovative ideas. He helped President Diem overcome serious challenges and solve thorny problems of national importance. He was consulted on every aspect of government, and no important decision was ever made without his participation. His influence was such that all cabinet ministers sought his guidance before taking action. It was also Mr. Nhu who gave birth to personalism and the Strategic Hamlet program. During indoctrination sessions, he gave lectures to cabinet ministers and high-ranking military and civilian officials on subjects relating to strategy and even tactics. With the death of the Ngo brothers, South Vietnam had lost two prominent leaders whose stature and capabilities had enabled the nation to face its communist foes with self-assurance.

But because of their towering authority, military leadership in the RVNAF had no chance to develop, especially at the higher levels. The military situation also posed no major challenges as the RVNAF devoted all their efforts to reorganization and training. The RVNAF commanders, therefore, did not have good opportunities to assert their leadership qualities and talents.

The period of the National Leadership Committee can be viewed as a period of crisis in leadership. The death of President Diem resulted in such a void in leadership that no one among the victorious generals could take his place. National leadership, therefore, broke down into factions that fought among themselves for ascendancy. The crisis was resolved by instituting collective leadership and a division of power and authority among the generals. But this seemed to satisfy no one, especially the more ambitious. Furthermore, collective leadership weakened the RVNAF command and control, and for some time, confusion reigned throughout the military hierarchy because no military commander was sure to whom he could give orders and from whom he could take orders.

This confusion turned into a serious crisis when some field commanders hid behind the growing power of militant Buddhist leaders to defy central authority. The fact that three successive recalcitrant corps commanders had to be removed testified to the debilitating weakness of collective leadership and the ineffectiveness of military leadership when mixed with politics.

During this period, the RVNAF performed the secondary role of supporting pacification and development, a role that did not lend itself to distinction and prominence. However, because of the lessened combat burden, the RVNAF were able to make good progress in force structure development and training. More emphasis was also placed on leadership training, especially at the small-unit level, and more efforts were expended to further consolidate the training base and improve the selection of personnel. At the same time, however, corruption became an issue of concern and somewhat tainted the reputation of the military. It seemed that in addition to professional competency, a successful RVNAF commander was also required to be honest and incorruptible. Integrity and moral rectitude, therefore, became the foremost traits sought after in military leadership.

The Second Republic was a period of big challenges that thoroughly tested both national and military leadership. The advent of elective democracy removed politics from the RVNAF and strengthened military command and control. Therefore, despite an inflationary economy, social vices, and internal dissent, the period saw the emergence of aggressive and strong military leadership from corps down to small units. This leadership seemed to grow and mature professionally despite great adversity. Throughout the major challenges they had to face, RVNAF commanders successfully carried out increasingly difficult tasks in a most commendable manner.

Despite the RVN-U.S. military success in defeating the enemy's 1968 Tet offensive, an important development occurred which had a far-reaching impact on the conduct of the war. Initiated under the Nixon Doctrine, the Vietnamization program represented an important turn in American foreign policy toward South Vietnam. For unknown reasons, the RVN leadership never took any course of action designed to meet this new challenge, aside from objecting to Vietnamization as a term. The national leadership appeared to adhere to an inflexible, obsolescently orthodox policy and failed to plan for political and diplomatic contingencies that might arise as a result of the new situation. In terms of political wisdom and sagacity, this was a far cry from the period of the First Republic.

Some people may incidentally ask: what would Mr. Diem and Mr. Nhu have done had they still been in power and how would they have approached the problem of facing the Communists without Americans? It is a difficult question to answer, but many believed that they would have taken some appropriate action. They remember that during 1963, as Mr. Diem and Mr. Nhu realized that Americans were becoming less friendly to the regime and appeared willing to abandon them, Mr. Nhu reportedly contacted the Communists to negotiate a modus vivendi in an attempt to reverse what he saw as an unfavorable situation. Whatever Mr. Nhu did in 1963 still remains a speculation, but it shows that, regardless of the consequences, a national leader must always look ahead of his times, plan for contingencies and meet new challenges in a flexible manner.

The RVNAF leadership, however, proved it had come of age, especially during the 1970 Cambodian incursion, the first major test of Vietnamization. Strong and dedicated leadership enabled III and IV Corps to achieve great success during the operation and set an example in which the RVNAF could take pride. It was only unfortunate that such excellent leaders as Generals Tri and Thanh had found their promising careers cut short by accidental death. I Corps, however, fared less well during the crossborder operation into lower Laos. The apparent lack of strong leadership deprived this major ARVN command of a chance to prove its full capabilities.

The same lack of strong and effective leadership led to the initial setback of I Corps during the 1972 Easter Offensive. Had I Corps had a better arrangement for command and control, perhaps Quang Tri would not have been lost despite the ferocity of enemy attacks. The example I have provided concerning I Corps during its counteroffensive amply proves that leadership did make a difference. Why else would a corps commander succeed where another had failed if not because of superior leadership? But men like General Truong were rather the exception among ARVN corps commanders. In fact during its entire existence, South Vietnam did not produce very many leaders like him. I believe that if II Corps had been led by someone like General Truong, perhaps it would not have met with such a tragic fate at the time of its redeployment during the final enemy offensive in 1975.

As a challenge to RVNAF leadership, the 1972 offensive also provided the opportunity for other commanders to prove their talents. An Loc had held against extreme odds partly due to U.S. air support but also because its commander refused to yield to overwhelming pressure. And this inspired his men to fight on despite privations and hardship. Kontum was another example of resourceful and dedicated leadership at the division level. The merit of its successful defender lay in the fact that he was an aggressive commander who knew how to use his resources and trained his subordinates well.

The cease-fire agreement of January 1973 ushered South Vietnam into an unfavorable situation which demanded flexibility and resourcefulness in dealing with an archenemy. But the RVN leadership failed to come to grips with reality and maintained a position which proved untenable as soon as U.S. military aid was cut back. During this period the RVNAF overextended themselves and found it hard to counter intensifying enemy violations effectively without United States support. In spite of their dedication, ARVN commanders felt less self-assured in the absence of U.S. advisers and support. The prevailing mood was one of uncertainty and false hope in the face of mounting enemy buildup.

Internal dissension and growing demands for the elimination of corruption cornered President Thieu into removing some of the better field commanders and replacing them with those of dubious courage and dedication. The choice he made was indeed a hard one and perhaps against his own will. It proved disastrous in mid-March 1975 when a troop redeployment of strategic proportions on which he had relied to save the situation ended in failure because of poor and unreliable leadership. The ensuing collapse of South Vietnam, in the final analysis, was also the accumulated failure of a leadership which did not see for itself all the implications of changing policies and take action in time.

In retrospect, we have to admit that despite this failure, both the national and military leadership of South Vietnam did make serious efforts in the performance of their roles. But these efforts were impeded not only by the debilitating effect of a protracted war and a divisive society but also by certain external factors beyond their control. To survive, the nation certainly needed unlimited resources and superior leadership. Unfortunately, the ill fate of South Vietnam had wanted that it should have neither.

Of the flaws and vulnerabilities that military leadership in the RVNAF might have demonstrated, the most detrimental were perhaps political-mindedness and corruption. The November coup of 1963 had changed military leadership so completely that the RVNAF were never the same again. Its effect could still be felt even after elective democracy had been institutionalized. Politics had been so ingrained among senior commanders that it was impossible for them to relinquish it and return to military professionalism. The Thieu regime, in fact, feared not so much the enemy from the outside as those who had once been partners and comrade-in-arms. And that explained why, one by one, the politically-ambitious ones had to go, but potential rivalry still persisted.

As to corruption, although it was not directly accountable for the collapse of the nation, its effect certainly debilitated professional competency and by extension, the war effort. The regime eventually accepted corruption as an inevitable vice because, as Vice President Huong had tragically admitted, "we would be left with practically no one to fight the war if all corrupt commanders were to be prosecuted and relieved." This also explained why despite its efforts, the JGS was never able to purge corruption from the RVNAF ranks. Many, therefore, seemed resigned to the idea that between the two evils, the choice had to be the lesser one. Although hard evidence was usually difficult to obtain, the finger seemed to be pointing primarily at the province chiefs who, as a special breed of commanders, enjoyed both military and civilian prerogatives while hardly submitting to the direct control of either.

As a country which was not only underdeveloped but also ravaged by a vicious war and under the constant threat of communist subversion in its own backyard, perhaps South Vietnam needed a special kind of leadership. Western principles of leadership are tailored to stable, truly democratic societies which usually require of their military leaders little else than professionalism. This presupposes ideological unity and loyalty to the national leadership, which are perhaps taken for granted in Western societies but are the very things that South Vietnam strived hard to achieve without great success. Therefore, steadfast anti-Communism and dedication to the national course had always been the primordial criterion in the selection of personnel slated to hold key positions in the RVNAF military hierarchy. In the exercise of leadership, most RVNAF commanders found these guidelines desirable in addition to military professionalism.

What then should be required of military leaders as most desirable traits? Again, the fourteen traits described as most desirable in Western societies and military organization are perfectly valid, especially when no serious social problems are involved. In the South Vietnamese society where traditions still made up the foundation of social life, such values as moral rectitude and personal conduct were also considered desirable in most leaders. Then, the widespread social vices of corruption and graft also made honesty and incorruptibility equally desirable qualities in the eyes of the South Vietnamese people, much more so in fact than the concept of integrity valued in Western leaders. Finally, a successful leader in the ideological context of the Vietnam war had to be someone who shared the lot of the common people and lived a material life not too far above theirs.

During the decade I served as chairman of the RVNAF Joint General Staff, I had witnessed all the successes and failures of our leadership. Even though this leadership had done its best, it still proved inadequate for this most difficult episode of our nation's history. And this explains to some extent the final failure of South Vietnam. Perhaps the survival of our nation would have required someone like a latter-day Tran Hung Dao or Nguyen Hue. The lack of such outstanding leadership indicates how destructive the long war had been in its heavy toll of young and promising leaders and how ravaging the French repressions against Vietnamese nationalists.

That one generation of leaders had failed does not necessarily mean that the way to success had been irretrievably blocked. Looking ahead into the future, there seems to be less cause for pessimism and despair. According to press reports and refugee accounts, the armed resistance against the new communist regime in South Vietnam is gaining momentum. Although it is a long and uphill struggle, the resistance has earned the respect and admiration of all Vietnamese living in exile. But for this armed struggle to succeed, there is an obvious and urgent need for outside assistance and support in every aspect in addition to the resistance movement's efforts to survive, fight, and expand on its own. Whoever the leaders of that movement may be, they certainly represent a new generation of emergent leadership of unprecedented self-abnegation, sacrifice and devotion. From the lessons learned during the lost war and with support from the outside, this emergent leadership has all the chances to succeed where the old one had failed. In this perspective, perhaps the resistance is not an utopia at all, despite some arguments to the contrary.

I conclude this monograph on a note of hope and with prayers for the reemergence of a free South Vietnam in the not too distant future, a South Vietnam led by men of talent and high morals—the truly great leaders of Vietnamese history.

Appendix A

JUSPAO FIELD MEMORANDUM
No. 38
May 30, 1967
Distribution: Standard

JUSPAO PLANNING OFFICE
SAIGON, VIET NAM

APPROVED BY: DIRECTOR
JUSPAO

SOURCES OF VIETNAM'S NATIONALIST TRADITION

The long drawn-out insurgency in South Vietnam and the country's troubled recent history as an object of colonial ambitions sometimes leave a foreign observer with the impression that the patriotic spirit on a sense of commitment to the national cause has become greatly attenuated. It is true that national traditions have until recently been neglected in the education of the urban elite in favor of western concepts and that the current encounter with the West has tended to focus attention on the consumer goods and convenience of a modern mass culture, but it would be entirely mistaken to undervalue the sense of nationhood and the national spirit that has imbued the Vietnamese in the course of the nation's history.

It is important for U.S. psyops personnel to show sympathetic understanding and provide assistance where appropriate for the continuing effort of the GVN to foster and fortify among the younger population the kind of patriotic spirit that can be mobilized for national aims. This educational effort is underway in the schools and through the mass media by renewed emphasis on the feats of patriots, poets and national leaders who distinguished themselves in the nation's long struggle for survival and independence. The hardy traits of earlier Vietnamese of whom the nation is justly proud stand out clearly in the two main thrusts of Vietnamese history: the centuries of resistance to powerful and covetous neighbors and the expansion southward to the Gulf of Siam, conquering and colonizing en route the kingdoms of the Champa and Khmer.

A striking manifestation of this indomitable national spirit was the complete defeat in the 13th century of the Golden Horde which had reined unchecked through Europe and Asia and had put much of the known world under the heels of the Mongol Emperor.

Twice in a single generation, in 1285 and in 1288, the Mongol forces commanded by That Hoan, King of Yunnan, son of Kublai Khan, were decisively beaten by the outnumbered Vietnamese army under Prince Tran Hung Dao, the uncle of the Tran Emperor Nhan Tong. Tran Hung Dao inspired the will to resist the invaders at the national congress called by Emperor Nhan Tong at the palace of Dien Hong to debate submission or resistance to the terrible horsemen from the North. "If your Majesty desires to surrender," he told Nhan Tong, "you will have to cut off my head first!" And to his officers he launched the <u>Proclamation</u>, excerpted below in free translation, which is one of the masterpieces of Vietnamese literature. The violent tone of the appeal combining calculated slurs on the reputation of his soldiers with a heady vision of victory, stirred the army into unprecedented action. His officers and men tattoed "Sat That" (Death to the Mongols) on their forearms and in a series of brilliant victories stopped the Mongol Army of half a million men in their tracks and expelled them from the country. The fate of the Khan's forces was sealed in 1288 at the river battle of Bach Dang in Kien An Province. In commemoration of this victory, the Vietnamese Navy has chosen Tran Hung Dao as their special patron, but his exploits speak to the hearts of all Vietnamese and temples are dedicated to his cult in Saigon (Hien Vuong street) and elsewhere throughout the country.

Tran Hung Dao Day is celebrated every year on the 20th day of the 8th Lunar Month, which in 1967 falls on September 23rd.

Psyops personnel will find it useful in their contacts with Vietnamese counterparts to be informed on Tran Hung Dao and show the respect due the nation-building feats of this medieval hero. Future papers in this series will be devoted to Le Loi, Le Van Duyet and the organizers of the intellectuals' revolt against European colonialism around the turn of the century.

ENCLOSURE

PROCLAMATION TO MY OFFICERS
by
Tran Quoc Tuan, Prince of Hung Dao (1284 AD)
(condensed and freely translated from the original)

"I have often read the history of our ancient heroes who sacrificed their lives to save their country. Had they been of faint heart and passed from the world under their own windows, their names never would have been inscribed on the rolls of silk to live eternally among us.

But you, the descendants of warriors, are little versed in the history of letters and might not entirely believe the feats of the past. Let me tell you therefore of more recent events:

We have seen the light of day in a time of troubles and have grown to manhood while the country has been in danger. We see the envoys of our enemies pridefully traveling our roads, jabbering in their tongue of owls to insult the Court; contemptible as dogs, they dare heap scorn on our dignitaries. Inflated with the power of the Mongol Sovereign and the support of his son, the King of Yunnan, they incessantly demand our tribute in gold and silver, in silks and precious pearls. Our treasury is limited, but their greed infinite. To appease it is like throwing meat to a famished tiger; it merely postpones the mortal peril.

Smitten by this calamity of our country I eat not in the daytime, nor can I sleep at night; my tears inundate my cheeks and my heart bleeds as if it were cut into pieces. I tremble with rage not yet to devour the enemy, to repose on his skin, to taste his blood. If it were necessary for this end that my corpse be burned a hundred times on the battlefield or a thousand times sewn into horsehide, happily would I consent and without regrets.

You have served for long in the army under my orders. When you lacked clothing I dressed you, when you needed rice I fed you, when your grades were low I promoted you, when your pay did not suffice I gave you silver. When you traveled on water I furnished you boats, on land I gave you horses. In war we shared the dangers, at great feasts our laughter mingled together. None of the ancient generals had more affection and solicitude for their officers than I have for you.

But what of you? You rest at ease while your sovereign is humiliated, indifferent while your country is disgraced. You, officers, serve the foreign barbarians and feel no sense of shame. You listen to the ceremonial music offered their ambassadors and do not burst of rage! No indeed; you amuse yourselves in cockfights, in the gambling tents, you enjoy your gardens and ricefields and the affection of your wives and children. The comfort of your possessions has permitted you to forget your duties to the State; the distractions of the fields and the hunt have made you neglect your military training, and some of you have been seduced by the pleasures of alcohol and the soft music of entertainers.

But will the spur of your cocks pierce the enemy's armor, or your tricks at cards serve to repel him? Will the yield of your gardens and fields suffice to pay your ransom or the affection of your wives and children save you from the enemy army? Your wealth is not enough to buy the enemy's will, nor can he be subdued by your wine and music.

Thus we all, you and me, will be made prisoners. Shame on our heads. And it will not only be my fief that I will lose, but your commissions that will pass into the hands of others. Not only my family that will be hunted down, but your wives and children reduced to slavery, not only the tombs of my ancestors trampled underfoot by the invader, but those of yours that will be desecrated. I will be humiliated in this existence and in a hundred others to come, my name will be sullied forever, but so will it be for yours and the honor of your families will be stained always by the shame of your defeat. Tell me, can you be happy with this in mind, even if you crave happiness?

In truth I tell you: take heed, as you would in stacking wood near the hearth, or in sipping a scalding goblet! Make of your soldiers experts in handling the bow and arrow as the ancient heroes, so that the head of Kublai Khan may be impaled before the gates of the Imperial Palace and the corpse of the King of Yunnan salted in a pannier of straw. Thus not only my fief will be consolidated forevermore, but your appointments assured in eternity; not only my family will enjoy the fruits of peace, but you will grow old surrounded by the warmth of your wives and children; not my ancestors alone will be honored through ten thousand generations; but yours will receive the ordained rites every spring and autumn; not only will I realize my purpose in this existence, but your reputation will survive a hundred centuries; not only will my name live in the memory of men, but yours, also, will pass into history. Can you wish more for perfect happiness?

I have consulted all the tracts on the arts of war to write the "Elements of Strategy". If you make an effort to study them and to follow my teachings, you will be my faithful companions. But if you neglect them and scorn what I have to say, you will become my enemies.

Why? Because the Mongols are our mortal foes. We cannot live with them under the same sky! Not to dream of cleansing the shame they inflict upon us, not to nourish in our hearts the resolution to destroy them, not to drill our soldiers to vanquish them, is to surrender. If this be your intention, you would leave behind you a name soiled for ten thousand generations, and once the enemy has been defeated, how can you ever carry your head high between heaven and earth?

   The purpose of this proclamation is to share with you my innermost thoughts."

Appendix B

```
                                        REPUBLIC OF VIETNAM
                                        MINISTRY OF DEFENSE
                                        JOINT GENERAL STAFF
TD 44-1                                       R.V.N.A.F.
11 September 1966                       ADJUTANT GENERAL DIVISION
```

SMALL UNIT COMMANDER'S HANDBOOK
1966

COUNTRY - HONOR - DUTY

THE RVNAF SOLDIER'S FIVE MORAL CODES

1. I am determined to sacrifice myself for the Country, Honor and Duty

2. I am resolved to defend the law and observe military discipline

3. I sincerely respect the old, love children, and behave correctly towards women; maintain a friendly attitude toward the people, help them, and defend them

4. I am resolved not to debauch myself through drinking, gambling, love affairs, and opium-smoking

5. I will absolutely preserve military secrecy; safeguard military equipment; and behave properly towards prisoners.

COMMAND AND LEADERSHIP DEPEND UPON:

LEADERS

THOSE WHO ARE LED

CIRCUMSTANCES

Preface

The Republic of Vietnam Armed Forces Joint General Staff has distributed this "SMALL UNIT COMMANDER'S HANDBOOK" with the purpose of reminding You of the essentials for improving the art of COMMAND AND LEADERSHIP.

COMMAND and LEADERSHIP, the responsibilities of the CADRE, must be continuously practiced, everywhere, in every circumstance, in every field. In fact, all daily tasks need your abilities for Reasonable and Timely Solutions. The cadre commanding low-level units are the Backbone of the Armed Forces. Each of your authoritative gestures and clear-sighted decisions reflects the Maturity of the cadre, instills Confidence in your subordinates, and certainly brings Success to your unit.

For the objectives mentioned above, the Joint General Staff hopes that this handbook will be always a loyal friend to help You accomplish the Noble and Difficult but Glorious Mission of the Leader on the path of service to the Armed Forces and the Country.

Introduction

Small Unit Commanders,

COMMAND AND LEADERSHIP is an art. This art materializes through the admiration shown by subordinates, when they are skillfully led, towards their leader. It is also the integration of self-knowledge, knowledge of one's subordinates, planning, clear-sighted action and determination on the part of the Commander.

Each leader is a representative of law and authority. He receives from higher authorities a mission on behalf of his comrades-in-arms under his command and combines his effort with those of his comrades-in-arms in conducting the fight to accomplish this mission under any circumstance and at any place. With this difficult and delicate responsibility, you must exert every effort to win the respect and loyalty of your subordinates, be the motivating force which pushes them to obey your orders to the letter, voluntarily accept responsibility, and carry out the mission until completion, regardless of hardship and danger. Loyalty and Admiration only manifest in your subordinates when they feel proud of and have full confidence in your leadership on the battlefront as well as in the rear area.

Through your attitude, speech, and action since the day you assumed command of your unit, your subordinates may have been aware of your command capabilities. In time, higher authorities will evaluate your talent and capabilities through the achievement attained by your unit, your care for your subordinates, and their actions and behavior. Therefore, each one of your decisions must be made after careful consideration as a result of your thorough knowledge of the mission and your subordinates. When taking up an action, you must be determined and confident. A leader can decide and act in this way only when he has complete self-control. Self-control of the body will result in an authoritative bearing; Self-control of the mind will result in sound judgement; Self-control of emotion will result in self-confidence, courage, justice and kindness.

Small Unit Commanders,

    During more than twenty years of continuous fighting against aggression, with the indomitable tradition of our race, the Republic of Vietnam Armed Forces have gradually reached maturity in war. The cadre, more than anyone else, must prove to be worthy of the duty assigned him, serve enthusiastically with the understanding that "The unit fights effectively only under skillful leadership" in order to achieve the early accomplishment of our mission: exterminate the Communists and save the country.

    I wish all of you success.

                                            Lieutenant General Cao Van Vien
                                            Chief of Joint General Staff, RVNAF
                                            Signed and Sealed

ARE YOU WORTHY TO LEAD YOUR MEN?

Reflect upon these points to:

A. KNOW YOURSELF

   1. About Your Personality and Attitude

      Ask yourself these questions:

      a. Your outward appearance:

         - Are your head, neck, ears and haircut neat and clean?
         - Are your manners of walking, standing, and sitting imposing?

      b. Your uniform:

         - Are your clothes well pressed?
         - Are your shoes and belt buckle well polished?

      c. Your way of living:

         - Do you lead a dissolute life?

      d. Your manner of speaking:

         - Do you use coarse and curt language?

      e. Your behavior:

         - Are you sincere and understanding?
         - Are you too hot-tempered?
         - Are you too severe?
         - Are you too weak-willed?
         - Have you carefully weighed and pondered over the facts?
         - Do you depreciate other people?

   2. About your required qualities:

      a. Do you have endurance to bear hardship along with your men in all circumstances?

      b. Are you fair in dispensing rewards and punishments?

      c. Are you determined when making a decision and then do you carry it out resolutely?

      d. Are you courageous enough:

         - To lead an assault when meeting with danger?
         - To accept legitimate reprimands?

e. Are you <u>confident</u> to carry out orders from higher authorities as well as to assign jobs to your subordinates?

f. Do you always seek to <u>improve</u> your learning and military career?

g. Do you have <u>forethought</u> to prepare plans in advance for next tasks?

h. Will you assume <u>responsibility</u>?

- To carry out the mission faithfully and seriously?
- To seek and accept other secondary tasks?

B. KNOW YOUR MEN

In what areas and why?

1. <u>Their persons</u>: rank; full name; service number; military occupational specialty; conduct; health; so that you may correctly address your men and use the proper man in the proper place

2. <u>Their family situation and problems</u>, in order to do all you can to help your men solve them

3. <u>Their experience</u>, in order to use them according to their capabilities

4. <u>Their thoughts</u>, in order to use your own ideas to guide them

5. <u>Their knowledge about</u>:

   a. Politics, secrecy preservation, and countersubversive measures

   b. Duties towards themselves and towards their families

   c. Duties towards their comrades-in-arms; their superiors; their unit; and the country

   d. Punishment for breaches of military conduct and discipline

C. EDUCATE AND ENCOURAGE YOUR MEN

1. You must seek to know all that happens around them every day in order to be able to educate, encourage, and comfort them at any place and at any time

2. You educate them so that:

   a. They may thoroughly understand the national policies

   b. They may have an esprit-de-corps

   c. They may be vigilant against colonialists' and Communists' schemes

   d. They may be fully aware of their responsibilities

   e. They may hold honor in high esteem

   f. They may improve their knowledge

   g. They may perfect their qualities

3. You should always remember that punishment is the last measure to be resorted to. The first measure to reform your men is through education, and the most effective way of educating your men is that you must set good examples.

4. You encourage your men by:

   a. Extolling them before their comrades-in-arms

   b. Praising them

   c. Rewarding them

   d. Urging them

   In fact, encouragement is not limited to any fixed form, but a glance of the eyes, a smile, a friendly gesture of a commander is effective enough to push men under his command to advance with honor.

HOW DO YOU WIN YOUR SUBORDINATES' LOYALTY AND ADMIRATION?

Remember:

A. YOUR SUBORDINATES RESPECT AND ADMIRE YOU:

   1. <u>Not because of</u>:

      a. Your leniency, your indulgence

      b. Your partiality

      c. Your tolerance with mistakes

      d. Your leniency towards disobedient persons

2. <u>But because of</u>:

    a. Your knowledge of yourself and your subordinates

    b. Your forethought in working

    c. Your fairness and impartiality

    d. Your sincerity and open-mindedness

    e. Your constant consideration for them

    f. Your care for them

B. HOW MUST YOU CARE FOR THEM?

Look into these areas and ask:

1. <u>Clothing</u>: Do their clothes fit, are they adequate?

2. <u>Weapons</u>: Are their weapons in good condition and properly maintained?

3. <u>Food</u>: Is their food substantial and adequate? Are they on reduced rations?

4. <u>Quarters</u>: Are their quarter hygienic?

5. <u>Pay and allowances</u>: Are they paid regularly on time? Do they receive their additional allowances quickly?

6. <u>Leaves</u>: Are leaves granted at the proper time and equally to all personnel in the unit?

7. <u>Work</u>: Are their assignments beyond their ability? Are they overly tired?

8. <u>Health</u>: Is preventive medicine administered? Inoculations? Is medicine for malaria prevention taken?

9. <u>Mail</u>: Is mail delivered rapidly and adequately?

10. <u>Rewards</u>: Are their labors and services noted, and are they rewarded appropriately and within the proper length of time?

11. <u>Welfare</u>: Are their families well settled? Have their medical examination cards and commissary (PX) cards been issued yet? Can they easily purchase adequate commissary commodities to meet their needs? Are there schools for their children? Do they receive assistance and is their

grief or joy shared when they meet with misfortune, have funerals, weddings, births, etc.

C. ONCE THEY ARE LOYAL AND RESPECT YOU THEY WILL OBEY YOUR ORDERS IMMEDIATELY, VOLUNTEER TO ASSUME RESPONSIBILITIES, AND DO THEIR JOBS WELL UNTIL COMPLETION.

WHAT SHOULD YOU DO WHEN YOU ARE NEWLY ASSIGNED TO A UNIT?

Whether or not you are successful in commanding your unit, or in other words, whether you can win the loyalty and respect of your men or not depends primarily on the <u>first impression</u> you make on them.

So, what should you do?

A. WHEN YOU FIRST ASSUME COMMAND

1. You should pay attention to your <u>manner and bearing</u>, which will be reflected by:

    a. Your head, neck, crew-cut hair etc., being trim and neat

    b. Your neat, clean and well-creased uniform

    c. Your polished shoes and shining belt buckle

    d. Your erect posture, your face looking straight forward without glancing sideward

    e. Your correct, firm and unaffected way of saluting

    f. Your seriousness, calmness and self-confidence

2. <u>Speak loudly</u>, <u>slowly</u>, <u>clearly</u> and as <u>little</u> as you can: Your subordinates will look at you and judge you at this very time

B. AFTER ASSUMING YOUR COMMAND

1. You should <u>receive</u> your subordinates according to the order of their rank and function. What is the objective of this reception?

    a. To learn something about the individual himself. The Personnel Roster (QD830) and your notebook will provide you with all details (biographical data, family status, clothing, etc.)

    b. To learn your men's ideas of what is needed to improve the potential of the unit

    c. To know the performance of the unit, its victories as well as defeats

d. To familiarize yourself with daily activities of the unit

e. To ensure settlement of pay, posting and delivery of mail

2. You should visit and inspect various facilities: quarters, mess-hall, latrines, dispensary, arms room, ammo pit, barber shop, recreational facilities, common equipment (weapons, clothing, signal equipment), dependents' housing, defense and security system (sentry-box, gun emplacements, etc.)

3. You should draw up a plan for improving the unit's way of life, based on facilities available

4. Then prescribe a daily activities schedule for the unit to include: sleeping, getting up, meals, roll call, order of the day, training, studying, equipment maintenance, recreation, physical training

5. You should exercise control and supervision to have the activity schedule respected and correctly implemented

WHAT MUST YOU DO TO CONDUCT AN OPERATION?

A. PREPARATIONS

You should:

1. Carefully study the Operations Order, the Intelligence Annex and the maps

2. Issue orders to unit commanders to make preparations

3. Distribute a summarized report on the enemy situation and capabilities to your subordinates

4. Re-check all counter-intelligence measures to see whether they are effective or not

5. Issue accurate, concise, and clear orders

6. Check personnel and equipment:

    a. Make a roll call, record names in the Personnel Roster (Form QD830) and carry it along

    b. Carry along the Loss Report (Form QD831)

    c. Clothing, weapons and ammunition of each individual and the unit must be carried along

    d. Signal facilities (radio sets, batteries, etc.)

- e. Rations and cooking utensils must be carried along
- f. Bandages and medicines must be made available to individuals as well as to the first-aid station
- g. Insure that dog tags are worn

B. MOVEMENT TO THE BATTLEFIELD

It must be made:

1. Secretly
2. Quietly
3. Orderly
4. In a disciplined manner

"TROOPS MUST MOVE OUT TO THE BATTLEFIELD LIKE A CRAWLING SNAKE"

C. ON THE BATTLEFIELD

1. Always maintain the proper formation (advance guard, flank guard, and rear guard) to avoid being attacked by surprise
2. Coordinate firepower with troop movement
3. Make spot reports on enemy activities or activities relating to the enemy
4. Process captured prisoners of war immediately to collect tactical information on the spot
5. Attack forcefully and swiftly, and liquidate the objective as soon as possible before nightfall

"TROOPS MUST MOVE ON THE BATTLEFIELD LIKE LIGHTNING AND THUNDER"

DO YOU KNOW YOUR AUTHORITY?

A. WHAT IS AUTHORITY?

Authority is a means provided you by the government and the Armed Forces to enable you to accomplish the mission.

B. HOW TO USE IT?

1. You must use it impartially, justly, logically, timely, and resolutely

2. You should use it only when all other means such as education and training are no longer effective

3. Remember that punishment is used to warn others, not only to chastise an offender

C. YOUR AUTHORITY IN ENFORCING MILITARY DISCIPLINE

How much punishment you can mete out to your men depends on:

1. Your rank
2. Your function
3. The type of violation committed

Study the following *Tables 1, 2, and 3* carefully to ensure that you use your authority properly.

D. REGULATIONS CONCERNING THE IMPLEMENTATION OF PUNISHMENT

In addition to your authority, there are a few regulations you should know to ensure that the punishment is correctly implemented.

1. Concerning those undergoing punishment:

    a. Military personnel punished while the unit is in operation, will undergo their punishment when the operation is terminated

    b. Military personnel under treatment at a hospital will undergo their punishment upon their return to their unit

    c. Enlisted men undergoing punishment who must do fatigue-duty will do so in the day-time during and after working hours

    d. Because of service requirements, officers and NCO's to be punished may be required to do daily work during working hours and undergo their punishment at the Disciplinary Barracks after working hours and at night

2. If a command authority inflicts a maximum punishment less than the number of days prescribed, the punishment record will be referred to higher authorities for further determination.

3. With regard to breaches of military custom (long haircut, untidy uniform, failure to maintain clothing and equipment, dirty and rusty weapons, etc.) the offender's immediate superior (from squad leader up) will receive a punishment similar to that of the principal offender.

TABLE 1 —— PUNISHMENT AUTHORITY ACCORDING TO RANKS

AUTHORITY RECOMMENDING PUNISHMENT (a) 1	MAXIMUM PUNISHMENT (b) APPLICABLE TO			REMARKS 5
	Officers 2	NCO's 3	Enlisted men 4	
Corporal Corporal 1st Class			2 days of confinement to barracks	(a) Military personnel from Corporal to 1st Lieutenant may make recommendations to punish military personnel of lower ranks who are not their subordinates, by virtue of their direct punishment authority. (b) In case there are two or three different types of punishment which may be alternatively applicable, the authority who recommends punishment may choose only one of them for application
Sergeant Sergeant 1st Class		2 days of administrative restriction	4 days of confinement to barracks	
Master Sergeant Sergeant Major Sergeant Aspirant		4 days of administrative restriction	6 days of confinement to barracks 2 days of confinement to room	
Second Lieutenant	2 days of administrative restriction	6 days of administrative restriction	8 days of confinement to barracks 4 days of confinement to room	
First Lieutenant	4 days of administrative restriction	8 days of administrative restriction	10 days of confinement to barracks 6 days of confinement to room	
Captain With regard to military personnel of lower ranks who are not his subordinates	4 days of administrative restriction	8 days of administrative restriction	10 days of confinement to barracks 6 days of confinement to room	

1	2	3	4	5
Captain With regard to sub-ordinate military personnel	6 days of administrative restriction	10 days of administrative restriction 8 days of close confinement	12 days of confinement to barracks 10 days of confinement to room 8 days stockade	
Field grade officers, With regard to non-subordinate military personnel of lower ranks	6 days of administrative restriction	10 days of administrative restriction 8 days of close confinement	12 days of confinement to barracks 10 days of confinement to room 8 days stockade	
Major With regard to sub-ordinate military personnel	10 days of administrative restriction 8 days of close confinement	12 days of administrative restriction 8 days of close confinement	15 days of confinement to barracks 12 days of confinement to room 10 days stockade (c)	(c) Of which there may be 3 days of solitary confinement.
Lt. Colonel With regard to sub-ordinate military personnel	15 days of administrative restriction 12 days of close confinement	15 days of administrative restriction 12 days of close confinement	20 days of confinement to barracks 15 days of confinement to room 12 days stockade (d)	(d) Of which there may be 4 days of solitary confinement.

1	2	3	4	5
Colonel With regard to subordinate military personnel	20 days of administrative restriction 15 days of close confinement	20 days of administrative restriction 15 days of close confinement	25 days of confinement to barracks 20 days of confinement to room 15 days stockade(e)	(e) Of which there may be 5 days of solitary confinement
General officers With regard to non-subordinate military personnel of lower rank	20 days of administrative restriction 15 days of close confinement	15 days of close confinement	15 days stockade(e)	(f) Of which there may be 6 days of solitary confinement
Brigadier General With regard to subordinate military personnel	25 days of administrative restriction 20 days of close confinement 8 days of confinement under guard	20 days of close confinement	20 days stockade(f)	(g) Of which there may be 10 days of solitary confinement
Major General With regard to subordinate military personnel	30 days of administrative restriction 30 days of close confinement 15 days of confinement under guard	30 days of close confinement	30 days stockade(g)	(h) Of which there may be 13 days of solitary confinement
Lieutenant General With regard to subordinate military personnel	40 days of administrative restriction 40 days of close confinement 40 day of confinement under guard	40 days of close confinement	40 days stockade(h)	

1	2	3	4	5
General of the Army With regard to subordinate military personnel	50 days of administrative restriction 50 days of close confinement 50 days of confinement under guard	50 days of close confinement	50 days stockade (1)	(1) Of which there may be 16 days of solitary confinement

TABLE 2 —— PUNISHMENT AUTHORITY ACCORDING TO FUNCTIONS

AUTHORITY RECOMMENDING PUNISHMENT (a)	MAXIMUM PUNISHMENT (b) APPLICABLE TO			REMARKS
1	Officers 2	NCO's 3	Enlisted men 4	5
Company grade officers assuming the function of: (c)				(a) Authorities who recommend punishments must apply the authority to punish according to rank as specified in Table 1 and not according to functions as specified in Table 2.
Provincial group commander	10 days of administrative restriction	15 days of administrative restriction	15 days of confinement to barracks	
Sector commander				
Garrison commander	8 days of close confinement	10 days of close confinement	15 days of confinement to room	
Military school or training center commandant			10 days stockade (d)	
Field grade officers assuming the function of: (c)				(b) In case there are two or three different types of punishment which may be alternatively applicable the authority who recommends punishment may choose only one of them for application.
Troop unit commander	20 days of administrative restriction	20 days of administrative restriction	20 days of confinement to barracks	
Sector commander				
Garrison commander	15 days of close confinement	15 days of close confinement	20 days of confinement to room	
Military school or training center commandant				
Commander of brigade, division, special sector or DTA	25 days of administrative restriction	20 days of close confinement	15 days stockade (e)	(c) Term commonly used to designate any commander of a separate administrative organization or unit, (regimental commander, group commander, etc.)
Special Forces commander			20 days stockade (f)	
CALC commander	20 days of close confinement			
Service branch commander				
Director of central or service department				
Air Force, Navy commander				
Campaign commander	30 days of administrative restriction			(d) Of which there may be 3 days of solitary confinement
Corps commander	30 days of close confinement	30 days of close confinement	30 days stockade (e)	

1	2	3	4	5
CTZ commander	15 days of confinement under guard			(e) Of which there may be 5 days of solitary confinement
Combat arm commander	35 days of administrative restriction			(f) Of which there may be 6 days of solitary confinement
	35 days of close confinement			
	35 days of confinement under guard			
Chief of Staff, JGS, RVNAF		35 days of close confinement	35 days stockade (h)	(g) Of which there may be 10 days of solitary confinement
	50 days of administrative restriction			(h) Of which there may be 11 days of solitary confinement
	50 days of close confinement			
	50 days of confinement under guard			
Chief of the Joint General Staff, RVNAF		50 days of close confinement	50 days stockade (i)	(i) Of which there may be 16 days of solitary confinement
	60 days of administrative restriction			(j) Of which there may be 20 days of solitary confinement
	60 days of close confinement			
	60 days of confinement under guard			
Minister of Defense		60 days of close confinement	60 days of stockade (j)	

TABLE 3 — VIOLATIONS AND APPROPRIATE PUNISHMENTS

Description of offenses and circumstances under which offenses are committed	Duration and type of punishment			Pay reduction	Transfer	Disciplinary Board	Discharge for breach of discipline	Reduction in rank	Court Martial	REMARKS
	EM stockade close confinement	NCO close confinement	Officer close confinement							
1	2	3	4	5	6	7	8	9	10	11
A. BREACHES MILITARY CONDUCT										
1. Failure to salute superiors	4 days	8 days	10 days							
2. Impoliteness toward superiors	15 days	15 days	20 days							
3. Impoliteness toward superiors in public	30 days	40 days	40 days							
4. Untidy uniform	4 days	8 days	15 days							
5. Long haircut	4 days	8 days	15 days							
6. Illegal fishing or hunting	30 days	30 days	40 days							
7. Assault	8 days	10 days	15 days							
8. Assault and battery	20 days	20 days	30 days							
9. Resisting police	15 days	15 days	20 days							
10. Assaulting police	50 days	50 days	50 days							
11. Collective assault of police	50 days	50 days	50 days							
12. Seduction of a minor	30 days	30 days	30 days							
13. Adultery	30 days	30 days	30 days							
14. Rape	50 days	50 days	50 days							
15. Vagrancy, robbery	50 days	50 days	50 days							
16. Causing an accident while driving	15 days	20 days	20 days							
17. Fraud, breach of trust	40 days	40 days	40 days							
18. Gambling	20 days	20 days	40 days							
19. Misuse of clothing of other service branches	10 days	15 days	20 days							

1	2	3	4	5	6	7	8	9	10	11
20. Misuse of authority for private gains	10 days	15 days	40 days							
21. Embezzling POL and military equipment	40 days	40 days	50 days						x	
22. Abandonment of family	15 days	15 days	15 days							
23. Fraudulent impersonation	15 days	15 days	15 days						x	
24. Traffic violation	15 days	20 days	20 days							
B. VIOLATION OF MILITARY DISCIPLINE										
1. Disregarding chain of command	10 days	15 days	20 days							
2. Disregarding chain of command and addressing to the Chief of State or the Prime Minister	50 days	50 days	50 days							
3. Showing disrespect toward and assaulting superiors	50 days	50 days	50 days							
4. Beating or assaulting inferiors	50 days	50 days	50 days							
5. Repeat of above offense or causing serious injury	50 days	50 days	50 days							
6. Using EM for personal benefit	50 days	50 days	30 days							
7. Unlawful keeping of weapons	30 days	30 days	30 days						x	

1	2	3	4	5	6	7	8	9	10	11
8. False declaration of family status:										
a. Self confessed	40 days	40 days	40 days	x						
b. Discovered	50 days	50 days	50 days	x					x	
9. Embezzlement of public funds	50 days	50 days	50 days	x						
10. Misappropriation of EM mess funds	50 days	50 days	50 days	x					x	
11. Falsifying diploma or certificate	50 days	50 days	50 days		x			x	x	
12. Absent without leave:										
a. First offense	one day Abs: 2 days " 3 "	as in the left column -"-	as in the left column x	x	x					This period of absence without leave will not be used in the computation of seniority, as regards EM. Not authorized to attend school. Promotion will be delayed for one year.
b. Recurrence one within a one-year period	-"-	-"-	-"-							
c. Three periods of absence within a 2-year period	-"-	-"-	-"-	x	x	x		x(a)		
13. Reporting late to new unit without a letitimate reason	One day Abs: 2 days	as in the left column	as in the left column	x						
14. Neglect of duty	10 days	15 days	20 days							
15. Failure to carry out commander's orders	10 days	15 days	20 days							
16. Dodging combat operation	50 days	50 days	50 days							
17. Failure to obey orders during combat operations	50 days	50 days	50 days		x		x	x		
18. Failure to maintain military clothing and equipment	10 days	15 days	20 days							
19. Acting as fifth columnist for the enemy (b)	50 days	15 days	20 days				x	x	x	

(a) Not applicable to officers
(b) To be handed to national police for proper security measures.

1	2	3	4	5	6	7	8	9	10	11
20. Failure to report a comrade whom he knows is working for the enemy	50 days	50 days	50 days	x	x				x	
21. Failure to report to higher authorities when being proselytized by the enemy	40 days	40 days	40 days		x		x			
22. Having a previous record of activities for the enemy (No proof of contact)	30 days	40 days	50 days							

WHAT SIGNS INDICATE THAT YOUR UNIT IS WELL LED?

Your unit is well led when

A. YOU AND ALL YOUR MEN:

   1. Are courteous, cheerful, neat, clean and well dressed

   2. Are thoroughly familiar with the rules of individual and team combat

   3. Have initiative, pride, a spirit of individual and team competition

   4. Work enthusiastically as a team

B. WEAPONS, CLOTHING, AND EQUIPMENT:

   1. Are in good condition

   2. Are carefully and properly maintained

C. BARRACKS:

   1. Are in good order

   2. Are clean

   3. Are artistically decorated

D. RECORDS OF INDIVIDUALS AND THE UNIT:

   1. Are kept up-to-date

   2. Are timely prepared

   3. Are accurate

MACAG Translation Division Log.
Nr. 4158

Glossary

ABN	Airborne
APC	Armor Personnel Carrier
ARVN	Army of Vietnam. The common term used to refer to regular army forces to include airborne and ranger units
CBU	Cluster Bomb Unit
CIDG	Civilian Irregular Defense Group
CMD	Capital Military District
COMUSMACV	Commander, U.S. Military Assistance Command Vietnam
CP	Command Post
CTZ	Corps Tactical Zone. The geographical area of responsibility of a Corps, but frequently and erroneously used to refer to the Corps headquarters itself: e.g. "CTZ will review ...," DTA will submit to CTZ ..." The term "Region" is sometimes used interchangeably with CTZ since both encompass the same geographical area
DMZ	Demilitarized Zone
DTA	Division tactical area. The geographical area of responsibility of a division (prior to 1970).
FANK	Forces Armees Nationales Khmeres (Khmer National Armed Forces)
FWMAF	Free World Military Assistance Forces
FY	Fiscal Year
GTA	Graphic Training Aid
GVN	Government of South Vietnam. Used to refer to the national government, to the entire governmental structure, or as an apposition to indicate one of its agents or agencies

HNC	High National Council
JGS	Joint General Staff (RVNAF)
LAW	Light antitank weapon
LCU	Landing Craft, Utility
LTL	Lien Tinh Lo (Interprovincial Route)
MAAG	Military Assistance Advisory Group
MACV	Military Assistance Command, Vietnam
MAP	Military Assistance Program
MASF/MILCON	Military Assistance Service Funded/Military Construction
MR	Military Region
MRC	Military Revolutionary Council
NCO	Non-Commissioned Officer
NDC	National Defense College
NLC	National Leadership Committee
NLF	National Liberation Front (VC)
NVA	North Vietnamese Army
PRG	Provisional Revolutionary Government (VC)
QL	Quoc Lo (National Route)
RD	Revolutionary (or Rural) Development
RF	Regional Forces
RVN	Republic of Vietnam
RVNAF	Republic of Vietnam Armed Forces. Refers to all three services
TF	Task Force
TOW	Tube-launched, Optically-tracked, Wire-guided
TRIM	Training Relations Instruction Mission
UBC	United Buddhist Church
UMDC	United Mobiles de Defense de la Chretiente (Mobile Units for the Defense of Christianity)
VNAF	Vietnamese Air Force
VNQDD	Vietnamese Nationalist Party (Kuomintang)